Read This...™ When I'm Dead

A GUIDE TO
GETTING YOUR
STUFF TOGETHER
FOR YOUR
LOVED ONES

By Annie Presley & Christy Howard

Read This...™ When I'm Dead
by Annie Presley & Christy Howard

Fourth Edition

Printed in the United States of America

ISBN: 978-0-9883425-7-6

www.booksbyace.com

ACE Publishing, LLC
KANSAS CITY, MO

Welcome To The Story of Your Life

The purpose of this book is to inform, entertain, and provide a format for you to compile information that matters to you and your loved ones. It is sold with the understanding that the publisher and authors are not engaged in rendering legal, accounting, or other professional services. Legal and financial planning/estate planning services should be sought from a competent professional.

Every effort was made to ensure that all information contained in this book was accurate and up-to-date at the time of publication. This text should be used only as a general guide and not as the ultimate source of information. **This does not take the place of a will. We encourage you to use this to help organize your thoughts as you consider your will.**

The authors and ACE Publishing, LLC shall have neither liability nor responsibility to any person or entity with respect to any loss or damage caused, or alleged to have been caused, directly or indirectly, by the information contained in this book, or by compiling personal information in this book.

This book should be kept in a safe location with other valuable and confidential documents, papers, and passwords.

This Book Contains Information About Me

NAME

ADDRESS

This book was filled out on ______________________________ (date)

It has been updated on the following dates:

Prepared For Your Eyes Only!

(List the people who should have access to the information in this book — keeping in mind your comfort with confidentiality.)

NAME PHONE NUMBER

NAME PHONE NUMBER

NAME PHONE NUMBER

NAME PHONE NUMBER

NAME PHONE NUMBER

NAME PHONE NUMBER

If you are not one of the individuals listed above, please immediately return this book to them!

This book is not a will. It is not a trust. It can, however, be used as a reference during the preparation of those documents.

Two very different experiences in the author's lives brought this book to life

Annie's thoughts:

After our parents' divorce, our fabulous mother died quite unexpectedly in my arms. I was 12 years old. My brother (13), our two-year-old sister, and I were lost without our mother's physical presence, and soft voice. On top of that, she did not leave behind anything to tell us about her – how she felt about us, her life, or her worldly treasures.

So very often I have wished that I could ask her a question… and talk to her about a million other things. If she had filled out a book like this, I would have some idea FROM her, ABOUT her… and about us.

Since that time, I have dealt with the deaths of other people I have loved. A book like this would have been of great value in each of those situations. I wrote this book so that other people would not have my experience.

My mom, two weeks before she died. June 1971.

Christy's thoughts:

I am the lucky mother of a wonderful 16-year-old daughter named Sommer. My mom was diagnosed with a rare disease when I was a 17-year-old freshman at Vanderbilt. The doctors thought she could survive 6 months. At her request, I tearfully remained in school and tried to come to grips with the fact that she would not be in my life much longer.

In my case, the story has a happy ending. It has been more than thirty years since that phone call, and my mother (one of my two best girlfriends – the other is my daughter) is still living! We have had decades to enjoy life together… and to prepare for her passing. I have told her "goodbye" many times when doctors predicted her imminent death. One of our favorite doctors, Jean Hausheer, warmly teases that my mom has more lives than a cat. Maybe we are a little crazy, but we laugh about it – because we have had these wonderful years we thought would be taken from us.

My daughter (Sommer) with my mom (Wanda) on Easter Sunday 2014.

My mother and I have dealt with the deaths of many other loved ones. Whenever there has been prior planning, the process is so much less difficult. The emotions are still keen, but when there is clarity about what to do, the grieving is based on the emotional loss, not on confusion or fear. I am fortunate that my mother has spent time organizing "things" for me so I will know what to do when she does finally transition from this life. It is time for me to begin that planning process for my own daughter.

When Annie mentioned that she wanted to create a book to help organize her "things and thoughts," I knew it was the right thing to do. I hope this book helps you organize your "stuff" and that you smile along the way.

Throughout this book, Annie and Christy share their thoughts and experiences.

Annie

Christy

Special thanks to our friends who provided input and personal stories along the way:

Frank Addington

Alison Coulson

Bob Deck

Katheigh Degen

Betsy Fentress

Courtney Fuchs

Laurie Ingram

Ada Koch

Sara Lewis

Merikay Lott

Shelley McThomas

Contents

PART ONE

My Personal Information

"I always wanted to be somebody. I see now that I should have been more specific."

Lily Tomlin

CHAPTER

1

It's All About Me

This chapter gives you the opportunity to share your family history, whether you were raised by your birth parents, adopted, lived in foster homes, or your parents divorced and you split time in various households.

Real life is complicated, lots of people can serve the role of "parent" in our lives!

References and Tips

1. This book is a good way to capture your genealogy for the purpose of tracking legal heirs and family connections. There are also websites and software that go into great detail. To see reviews and comparisons of genealogy search websites, go to www.genealogy-search-review.toptenreviews.com.

2. Be sure to include your past names. They really matter!

3. Not a tip, but worth knowing: Confucius' family tree spans 83 generations and includes 2 million people, although it is estimated that 3 million would be a more accurate number since some branches have been lost! He has been dead for 2500 years, and his family just keeps growing!

4. If you are interested in genographic information, which is a genetic family tree based on a sample of your DNA, look at:
   https://genographic.nationalgeographic.com
   http://www.dnaancestryproject.com
   www.familytreedna.com
   There are many others, and we don't endorse any of them specifically but you can search DNA family tree to get a list.

My mom gave me a DNA kit for Christmas. We had fun receiving the results, and kept checking the website for updates. I love that it is "stored" so that as more information from OTHER people is discovered, my own history becomes more complete.

My Names

NAME	DATE CHANGED	REASON FOR CHANGE

Be sure to include both nicknames and last names. Also remember to list names you have legally changed, as well as those you have used informally.

My birth name was Melissa Christine, but they called me "Christy." On some documents, I'm Melissa, on some I'm Christine, and on some I'm Christy!

The Longest Real Name We Could Find:

Adolph Blaine Charles David Earl Frederick Gerald Hubert Irvin John Kenneth Lloyd Martin Nero Oliver Paul Quincy Randolph Sherman Thomas Umcas Victor William Xerxes Yancy Zeus Wolfeschlegelsteinhausen Bergerdorff

Provided by http://www.omgfacts.com/lists/9076/The-longest-personal-name-ever-is-746-characters-long

How My Life Began

I was born in: ______________________________

city, county, state, country

Birth date: (including the year!) ______________________________

My name as it appears on my birth certificate: ______________________________

My birth certificate is located: ______________________________

Parents listed on my birth certificate:

Mother: ______________________________

Her maiden name was: ______________________________

Father: ______________________________

❑ I was raised by my birth mother and father for my entire youth. (If so, skip to page 20)

❑ I was not raised in the home of my birth parents for my entire youth.

The following pages give you the opportunity to explain where you lived.

My maternal grandmother was from a large family in South Dakota. They had very little money and in the 1920's one of her younger sisters went to live with another family for a period of time. All of my Grandmother's siblings shared one drawer of a cabinet that held all their clothing!

I Was Adopted

I was adopted when I was ________ days, ________ months or ________ years old.

The records can be found in ____

city, county, state, country

Name of adoption agency: ____

Address of adoption agency: ____

Name of attorney: ____

Address of attorney: ____

Adoptive parents: ____

Birth parents: ____

Take time to tell any story you wish to share, whether you have told it a million times or never before. Family history is important.

I Had Step Parents

❑ I lived with my father ______________________________ (name) and my step-mother.

Step-Mother: ______________________________

Her maiden name was ______________________________

She became my step-mother when she married my dad

on ______________________ in location ______________________
date

❑ I lived with my mother ______________________________ (name) and my step-father.

Step-Father: ______________________________

He became my step-father when he married my mom

on ______________________ in location ______________________
date

This is a good place to explain the living situation you experienced as a child/youth. Did you live only in one household, or did you split time between households?

I Had Foster Parents

Name of Foster Parent(s) ____

City/Address ____

My Age ____

We keep in touch today ____

____

____

You can explain your history here. Why were you in foster homes? Did you maintain contact with your birth parents? Did you have a favorite foster home? Did you have good or bad memories about any particular situation?

My School History

PRIMARY EDUCATION

Grade	School Name	School Address
Early Years		
Kindergarten		
First Grade		
Second Grade		
Third Grade		
Fourth Grade		
Fifth Grade		
Sixth Grade		
Seventh Grade		
Eighth Grade		
Ninth Grade		
Tenth Grade		
Eleventh Grade		
Twelfth Grade		

Special Primary School Memories or Honors

(be sure to list the grade)

My paternal grandfather almost finished 3rd grade before being called back to work as a sharecropper. My maternal grandmother was called back to work half way through her senior year of high school. Guess who was most mad about never finishing school?

Special Primary School Memories or Honors

(be sure to list the grade)

One of my favorite high-school experiences was singing in the choir with Mr. Zollars as our teacher. I was a "Chamber Singer" and I loved it. One of my WORST memories was the first day of sixth grade when I had to take the bus home for the first time…and there were so many buses lined up! I had no idea which one I was supposed to get on!

My College History

HIGHER EDUCATION

School Name and Address	Years Attended	What I Studied

My paternal grandfather studied law before there was an official law school named at his school. Educational structures change over time, so it could be very interesting for your family to understand your history much later! What we think of as "normal" today may look very different in years to come!

Special Higher Education Memories or Honors

(be sure to list the year)

My Marriage History

MY FIRST MARRIAGE

Name of Spouse ______________________ Date Married ______________

Location of Marriage (include the PLACE and the city and state) ______________

____

____

He/she is currently living ❑ yes ❑ no We are still married ❑ yes ❑ no

If not: He/she passed away on (date) ______________________

in (city and state) ______________________

OR

We were divorced on (date) ______________________

in (city and state) ______________________

We had or raised, biological, adopted or stepchildren together and their names are:

____

____

____

____

My Marriage History

MY SECOND MARRIAGE

Name of Spouse ______________________________ Date Married ____________________

Location of Marriage (include the PLACE and the city and state) ____________________

____

____

He/she is currently living ❑ yes ❑ no We are still married ❑ yes ❑ no

If not: He/she passed away on (date) ______________________________________

in (city and state) ______________________________________

OR

We were divorced on (date) ______________________________________

in (city and state) ______________________________________

We had or raised, biological, adopted or stepchildren together and their names are:

____

____

____

____

My Marriage History

MY THIRD MARRIAGE

Name of Spouse ______________________________ Date Married

Location of Marriage (include the PLACE and the city and state)

____

____

He/she is currently living ❑ yes ❑ no We are still married ❑ yes ❑ no

If not: He/she passed away on (date) ______________________________

in (city and state) ______________________________

OR

We were divorced on (date) ______________________________

in (city and state) ______________________________

We had or raised, biological, adopted or stepchildren together and their names are:

____

____

____

____

My Marriage History

MY FOURTH MARRIAGE

Name of Spouse ______________________________ Date Married

Location of Marriage (include the PLACE and the city and state)

____

____

He/she is currently living ❑ yes ❑ no We are still married ❑ yes ❑ no

If not: He/she passed away on (date) ______________________________

in (city and state) ______________________________

OR

We were divorced on (date) ______________________________

in (city and state) ______________________________

We had or raised, biological, adopted or stepchildren together and their names are:

____

____

____

____

My Job History

I HAVE WORKED FOR THE FOLLOWING COMPANIES/PEOPLE:

Company	Year Started	Year I Left	What I Did

My favorite job(s) was/were: ______________________________

____

____

The job I always wanted, or would have LOVED to try: ______________________________

____

Volunteerism / Memberships

Organization	Year(s)	My Involvement (Including any fun memories)

My paternal grandmother knit hats for premature babies well into her 90's. She made sure they were fun colors, and took them by the bag-full to the hospital. I can still see her smile and hear those knitting needles clicking as her time-worn hands created those much-needed caps!

Timeline

MY MEMORIES AND ACCOMPLISHMENTS

In my teens ______________________________

____

____

In my twenties ______________________________

____

____

In my thirties ______________________________

____

____

In my forties ______________________________

____

____

In my fifties ______________________________

____

____

Sometimes accomplishments relate to work or attaining physical or educational goals. I have a 10K in my future!

Timeline

MY MEMORIES AND ACCOMPLISHMENTS

In my sixties

In my seventies

In my eighties

In my nineties

In my hundreds

Don't forget the "emotional" accomplishments like forgiveness or healing wounds!

My Family Tree

In today's world, our family lineage is sometimes more complicated than you think. This section will help sort out any confusion that may arise. Go back as far as you can here. It could be important to your descendants!

PREVIOUS GENERATIONS

My Great-Great Grandparents

My Great Grandparents

Maternal Great Grandmother / Maternal Great Grandfather

Paternal Great Grandmother / Paternal Great Grandfather

Maternal Great Grandmother / Maternal Great Grandfather

Paternal Great Grandmother / Paternal Great Grandfather

My Grandparents

Maternal Grandmother

Paternal Grandmother

Maternal Grandfather

Paternal Grandfather

My Parents

Mom

Dad

My Siblings

My Family – The Details

MY ANCESTORS

My Mother's Family

My Family – The Details

MY ANCESTORS

My Father's Family

My Siblings

My Oldest Brother/Sister (circle one)

Name ____________________

This is my ❑ biological ❑ half ❑ step ❑ adopted ❑ foster sibling

His/her biological mother: ____________________

His/her biological father: ____________________

Other parents (explain): ____________________

____

____

Birth date: __________ Death date: __________

Current address is:

____

____

____

❑ Currently married (or if deceased, married to this person when died) to:

(Name) ____________________

____

This page allows you to list half or step siblings. (That gets clarified when you list the parents' names.) You can add extra details on the pages that follow!

My Siblings

My Oldest Brother/Sister - CONTINUED

❑ Not currently married (or if deceased, not married when died)

A lawyer told us about someone who died with no living children, no living parents, and no living siblings. The legal heirs were actually the siblings' children, who were extremely difficult to find. These pages could really help!

Previous spouses: ____________________________________

____

____

This brother/sister's children (my nieces/nephews) are:

____

____

____

____

____

Other important information about this sibling:

____

____

____

____

My Siblings

My Next Oldest Brother/Sister (circle one)

Name ____

This is my ❑ biological ❑ half ❑ step ❑ adopted ❑ foster sibling

His/her biological mother: ____

His/her biological father: ____

Other parents (explain): ____

____

____

Birth date: ______________________ Death date: ______________________

Current address is:

____

____

____

❑ Currently married (or if deceased, married to this person when died) to:

(Name) ____

We provided pages for up to four siblings. If you have more, please make a copy of these pages for the others!

My Siblings

My Next Oldest Brother/Sister - CONTINUED

❑ Not currently married (or if deceased, not married when died)

Previous spouses: ______________________________

____

____

This brother/sister's children (my nieces/nephews) are:

____

____

____

____

____

Other important information about this sibling:

____

____

____

My Siblings

My Next Oldest Brother/Sister (circle one)

Name ______________________________

This is my ❑ biological ❑ half ❑ step ❑ adopted ❑ foster sibling

His/her biological mother: ______________________________

His/her biological father: ______________________________

Other parents (explain): ______________________________

____

____

Birth date: ______________ Death date: ______________

Current address is:

____

____

____

❑ Currently married (or if deceased, married to this person when died) to:

(Name) ______________________________

My Siblings

My Next Oldest Brother/Sister - CONTINUED

❑ Not currently married (or if deceased, not married when died)

Previous spouses: ______________________________

____

____

This brother/sister's children (my nieces/nephews) are:

____

____

____

____

____

My twin sister died after our mother's LONG labor. (They would do a c-section today.) You might want to mention special situations here. I know I would mention Connie.

Other important information about this sibling:

____

____

____

My Children

My First-Born Daughter/Son (circle one)

(Name) ____________________

This child was born on ____________ (date) and died on ____________ (date)

This is my ❑ biological ❑ half ❑ step ❑ adopted ❑ foster sibling

Biological parents: ____________________

If adopted, we (myself and ____________________ name of the other parent)

adopted him/her on ____________ (date)

in ____________________ (city and state and country)

Give a brief history about this child's adoption or birth: ____________________

____

____

____

We left space for 6 children. If you have MORE than 6, copy one or two of the following pages!

Please note your child's critical information (e.g. food allergies, special requirements, doctors, medications, etc.)

____

____

____

____

My Children

Current address is ____

____

This child married: ______________________ (name) on ______________________ (date)

They are ❑ still married, or ❑ his/her spouse passed away on ____________________ (date)

❑ they divorced on ______________________ (date)

Previous spouses: ____

____

Additional notes about this child:

My Children

My Second-Born Daughter/Son (circle one)

(Name)____

This child was born on__________________(date) and died on __________________(date)

This was my biological or adopted or step-child. (Circle one.)

Biological parents:____

If adopted, we (myself and ____________________________ name of the other parent)

adopted him/her on ______________________(date)

in ______________________________________ (city and state and country)

Give a brief history about this child's adoption or birth: __________________________

____

____

____

Please note your child's critical information (e.g. food allergies, special requirements, doctors, medications, etc.)

____

____

____

____

These pages allow you to list step-children. (That gets clarified when you list the parents' names.) Consider them when you plan your estate. They may be your spouse's legal heirs, but not yours if you didn't adopt them! If you want them to inherit anything from you, you must be clear in your will or trust.

My Children

Current address is ____

____

____

This child married: ____________________ (name) on ____________________ (date)

They are ❑ still married, or ❑ his/her spouse passed away on ________________ (date)

❑ they divorced on ____________________ (date)

Previous spouses: ____

____

Additional notes about this child:

My Children

My Third-Born Daughter/Son (circle one)

(Name)____

This child was born on________________(date) and died on ________________(date)

This was my biological or adopted or step-child. (Circle one.)

Biological parents: ____

If adopted, we (myself and ________________________ name of the other parent)

adopted him/her on ____________________(date)

in ____________________________________ (city and state and country)

Give a brief history about this child's adoption or birth: ________________________

____

____

____

____

Please note your child's critical information (e.g. food allergies, special requirements, doctors, medications, etc.)

____

____

My Children

Current address is ______________________________

____

____

This child married: ______________ (name) on ______________ (date)

They are ❑ still married, or ❑ his/her spouse passed away on ______________ (date)

❑ they divorced on ______________ (date)

Previous spouses: ______________________________

____

Additional notes about this child:

My Children

My Fourth-Born Daughter/Son (circle one)

(Name)____

This child was born on________________(date) and died on ________________(date)

This was my biological or adopted or step-child. (Circle one.)

Biological parents: ______________________________________

If adopted, we (myself and ________________________ name of the other parent)

adopted him/her on ________________(date)

in __________________________________ (city and state and country)

Give a brief history about this child's adoption or birth:: ________________________

____

____

____

____

Please note your child's critical information (e.g. food allergies, special requirements, doctors, medications, etc.)

____

____

My Children

Current address is ____

____

____

This child married: ____________________ (name) on ____________________ (date)

They are ❑ still married, or ❑ his/her spouse passed away on ____________________ (date)

❑ they divorced on ____________________ (date)

Previous spouses: ____

____

Additional notes about this child:

Feel free to convert these pages to reflect your grandchildren as well.

My Children

My Fifth-Born Daughter/Son (circle one)

(Name)____

This child was born on__________________(date) and died on __________________(date)

This was my biological or adopted or step-child. (Circle one.)

Biological parents: ____

If adopted, we (myself and __________________________ name of the other parent)

adopted him/her on ____________________(date)

in ______________________________________ (city and state and country)

Give a brief history about this child's adoption or birth:: __________________________

____

____

____

____

Please note your child's critical information (e.g. food allergies, special requirements, doctors, medications, etc.)

____

____

My Children

Current address is ______________________________

____

____

This child married: ______________ (name) on ______________ (date)

They are ❑ still married, or ❑ his/her spouse passed away on ______________ (date)

❑ they divorced on ______________ (date)

Previous spouses: ______________________________

____

Additional notes about this child:

My Children

My Sixth-Born Daughter/Son (circle one)

(Name)____

This child was born on______________________(date) and died on ______________________(date)

This was my biological or adopted or step-child. (Circle one.)

Biological parents: ____

If adopted, we (myself and ____ name of the other parent)

adopted him/her on ___________________________(date)

in ____ (city and state and country)

Give a brief history about this child's adoption or birth:: _______________________________________

____

____

____

____

Please note your child's critical information (e.g. food allergies, special requirements, doctors, medications, etc.)

____

____

My Children

Current address is ____

____

____

This child married: ____________________ (name) on ____________________ (date)

They are ❑ still married, or ❑ his/her spouse passed away on ____________________ (date)

❑ they divorced on ____________________ (date)

Previous spouses: ____

____

Additional notes about this child:

Identifying Me

DOCUMENTATION

Birth certificate is located in ____________________

Marriage certificate(s) is/are in ____________________

Divorce decree(s) is/are in ____________________

Passport number is ____________________

My passport can be found in ____________________

Social Security number is ____________________

My Social Security card can be found in ____________________

Medicare number is ____________________

My Medicare Information can be found in ____________________

Medicaid number is ____________________

My Medicaid number can be found in ____________________

Veteran? Yes or No Branch ____________ Serial Number ____________

Inducted on ____________ at ____________________

Discharged on ____________ at ____________________

Final Rank ____________________

My previous 7 years tax returns can be found in ____________________

____

IMPORTANT Personal Information, like passports and your Social Security number should be stored in a secure location

Identifying Me

PHYSICALLY

My hair color is ______________________________

My eyes are (color) ______________________________

I do/do not wear dentures ______________________________

I do/do not wear contacts ______________________________

I do/do not wear glasses ______________________________

I weigh __________ pounds I am ______ feet and ______ inches tall

I have a mole on my ______________ in the shape of a __________

I have ______ (number) of gold teeth ______________

Piercings: ______________________________

Other physical identifiers (like a pin in your arm or a hip replacement):

____

____

I have a tattoo on my ______________ in the shape of a __________

____

____

____

____

This can be important if your loved ones need to identify you. We have all seen news shows about misidentification. This could help them in a time of grief when they are not thinking clearly.

IMPORTANT If you write personal, confidential information in this book, treat the book as you would treat that information! – Keep it safe and secure!

My Spiritual Journey

Share where you started, where you are now and where you are going on your spiritual journey.

Other Information I Want to Share

“In the end it’s not the years in your life that count. It’s the life in your years.”

Abraham Lincoln

CHAPTER

2

Just for Fun – Because Life Should be FUN!

Capture fun facts and memories here — the essence of you.

Five Tips for FUN:

1. Don't act your age!
2. Call a friend you haven't seen in a long time. Out of the blue.
3. Re-read a favorite book.
4. Learn a new card game with old friends.
5. Stop a bad habit.

Video Link or Story Keeper

❑ I have made a video for you to view. You can find the video

(web-site or physical location) ____

____

There are many ways to do this. Some ideas are:

1. If you have a computer with a camera, you can make a simple video on the computer and store it for your loved ones to view later.
2. If you have access to a video camera, you could set it up yourself or have a friend video you.
3. Some point & click cameras take videos, and most phones do, too. You can email them or put them on a thumb drive in a safe place (where they will be found).
4. Two places that walk you through making a video which you can email to others are: www.techsmith.com/jing/free and www.digitalfilms.com
5. Upload your video to www.youtube.com and share the link!

❑ I have not made a video

Be sure to specify where your video can be found if you have taken the time to make one for your loved ones!

Videos can be stored on a disc, on a computer, or online or in the cloud.

Highlights of My Life

Date	Event

When I Was in School

My best friends in grade school were: ____

____

____

My best friends in high school were: ____

____

____

My best friends in college were: ____

____

____

I studied ______________________ but wanted to study ______________________________

____

My first date was with ______________________ and we went to ______________________

____

____

____

When I was young, I worked at: ____

____

____

When I Was — A Young Adult (20's-30's)

My daily life went like this: ______________________________

____

____

____

My closest friends were: ______________________________

____

____

Some of my favorite things at this time of life were: ______________________________

____

____

____

____

Advice I'd give to someone that age: ______________________________

____

____

____

____

____

Mid-Life (40's and 50's)

My daily life went like this: ______________________________

____

My closest friends were: ______________________________

____

Some of my favorite things at this time of life were: ______________________________

____

____

My first mid-life crisis hit when I was ________ years old. I found myself doing

____

____

My second mid-life crisis hit when I was ________ years old. I found myself doing

____

____

Advice I'd give to someone that age: ______________________________

____

____

____

____

When I was... Mature (60's)

When I started to consider myself "mature" I was really ________ years old.

These are some of the things I thought about and did during that time.

My daily life went like this:

Advice I'd give to someone that age:

When I was Older (70's and Beyond)

My daily life went like this: ______________________________

These are some of the things I think about and do: ____________________

Advice I'd give to someone that age: __________________________

My Favorite Things

My favorite foods are: ____

____

My favorite sports teams are: ____

____

My favorite memories are: ____

____

____

My favorite music is: ____

____

My favorite movie stars are: ____

____

My favorite Presidents have been: ____

____

My favorite cities and countries are: ____

____

My other "favorites" are: ____

____

____

Family Lore

My famous ancestors were:

Name Famous for…

Any black sheep? Hmmm…

My relatives who should have been famous were:

Name Should have been famous for…

Tell a fun story from a previous generation.

My Bucket List

Activity	Date Accomplished

What I Never Told You...and Why

Family Recipes

Family Traditions

*“If your time ain’t come,
not even a doctor
can kill ya.”*

American Proverb

CHAPTER

3

Medical Mumbo-Jumbo

This chapter chronicles your health history for the benefit of your family and medical professionals who might need it.

Three Tips about Medical Mumbo Jumbo:

1. Keep excellent records about your health care. It gets confusing!
2. Your records are private, but it is a good idea to keep copies for yourself.
3. Recent articles have stated that genetic markers are less predictive than family history regarding health issues you may encounter.
4. Consider using a healthcare tracking app like www.MyMedicalApp.com

See Insurance chapter for medical insurance information!

My Medications

Medications I'm taking as I fill this out. (In case I am alive but unable to respond. So you can tell the medical team.) I've done my best to keep this updated, but call my doctors (listed on the following pages), too.

Name of Medication	Date	To Treat

My Medical History

Diseases/Illnesses (heart, lung, etc.) I Have Experienced

Diseases or Health Issues My Relatives Have Experienced

My Medical Timeline

Date	Medical Event, Diagnosis or Surgery

Hospice and Palliative Care

WHAT IS PALLIATIVE CARE?

Palliative care is designed for people who have serious illnesses. This type of care is not designed to cure your illness (curative treatment). Instead, palliative care focuses on improving your quality of life in your body, as well as your mind and spirit. Palliative care providers understand that serious illnesses can affect you and your loved ones.

WHAT IS HOSPICE?

Hospice is a program of care for people in the final phase of a terminal illness, focusing on comfort and quality of life. Hospice care can be provided either in the home, in a hospice facility, in nursing homes, or in hospitals. The goal is to provide support for the patient's emotional, social, and spiritual needs as well as enabling the patient to be free of pain and comfortable so that they may live their final days as fully as possible.

Hospice programs often include the services of a nurse, doctor, social worker and clergy in providing care. Sometimes physical therapy, musical therapy and speech therapy are provided. Trained volunteers may visit a patient during hospice. Respite programs are sometimes provided for the family of the terminally ill to provide the caregivers the opportunity to leave the house for a few hours. Volunteer care is part of the hospice philosophy.

Although hospice does not cure a terminal illness, hospice will sometimes provide medical treatment for ancillary conditions that can be cured (pneumonia for example).

THE HISTORY OF HOSPICE

The Latin word "hospitium" means guesthouse. The tem hospice was originally used to describe a place of shelter for tired or sick travelers returning from religious pilgrimages. During the 1960's, St. Christopher's Hospice near London was founded by Dr. Cicely Saunders. It was the first program to use modern pain management to provide compassionate care for the dying. In 1974, the first hospice program in the United States was established in New Haven, Connecticut. There are now thousands of hospice programs across the United States. Most insurance plans include hospice as a covered benefit. (Check with your provider.)

See National Hospice and Palliative Care Organization or www.NHPCO.org

Medical Contacts

MY HEALTH CARE PROVIDERS

Consider internal medicine, ophthalmologist (eye), ENT, pulmonologist, osteopath, allergy, oncologist, cardiologist, neurologist, psychiatrist, acupuncturist, chiropractor, podiatrist.

MY DOCTORS

Name	Specialty	Address	Phone Number

My Pharmacies

Name	Address	Phone Number

My Dentist

Name	Address	Phone Number

Let's examine the dog mind:
Every time you come home,
he thinks it's amazing.
He can't believe that you've
accomplished this again.
You walk in the door.
The joy of it almost kills him.
"He's back again! It's that guy!
It's that guy!"

Jerry Seinfeld

CHAPTER

4

The Poop on My Pets

Don't forget your animal friends. This can help you guide others on their behalf.

Tips To Help You Plan for Your Pets

1. Talk to friends now to determine whether they would be willing to care for your pet(s).

2. If you would like to compensate someone for caring for your pet, be sure to include that in your will or trust. You can also find information (for a fee) at http://www.nolo.com/legal-encyclopedia/question-provide-for-pets-pet-trust-28005.html, or at www.legalzoom.com (pet protection agreement).
   To determine which states currently allow pet trusts to be established and enforced, contact your state's attorney general or the Humane Society of the United States via www.hsus.org.

3. Keep in mind that annual costs for care vary with the health and age of the individual animal. Unless the person who takes your pet agrees to do it for free, you may need to offer to cover food, grooming, vet care and many other expenses. You may even want to factor in money to cover boarding the pet for those times that the caretaker cannot travel with animals. Obviously the dollars involved are dependent on the type of animal and the number of animals involved.

4. One summary document of things to consider can be found at: www.peaceofminddogrescue.org/lifetimecare.html

5. Love your pets!

Draw or attach a picture of your pet(s) here:

This section matters to me because of our beloved Sam. He was the rescue dog that brought our family together, and his ashes are still in our home. I'd love for his remains to join me in my final resting place.

Pet Plans

I have the following pets. Instead of taking them to a shelter or selling them, I would like them to be handled as follows:

Pet's Name ______________________________

Breed ____________________ Born ____________________

Vet ____________________ Phone Number ____________________

Medication ______________________________

I'd like ____________________ (name and phone number)

to care for this special pet because ______________________________

Health Concerns ______________________________

This pet's personal items are located ______________________________

❑ I have set aside money for the maintenance and care of this pet. ____________________

It is in account ____________________ at ____________________ (bank name)

located at ______________________________ (bank address)

(contact name) at ____________________ (phone number) can help you access these funds

❑ This pet is covered by pet insurance from ____________________ (company name)

at ______________________________ (address)

The policy number or identification number is ______________________________

Contact name: ____________________ and telephone number: ____________________

Pet Plans

❑ When this pet dies, if at all possible I would like his/her remains to be ________________

____

____

____

(Keep in mind that your wishes may not be possible, but you can at least explain your desires.)

____

❑ I would like this pet to participate in my funeral service as follows: ________________

____

____

(Be realistic here!)

Pet Preferences

Pet Name: ____

Food at: (am and pm) ______________________________

Treats ____

Toys ____

Bed ____

Kennel/Crate _____________________________________

Commands ____

Sleeps at night in the ______________________________

Pet Plans

I have the following pets. Instead of taking them to a shelter or selling them, I would like them to go to be handled as follows:

Pet's Name ____

Breed ________________________ Age __________________

Vet ________________________ Phone Number ______________

Medication ____

I'd like ______________________________ (name and phone number)

to care for this special pet because ____________________________

Health Concerns ____

This pet's personal items are located ____________________________

❑ I have set aside money for the maintenance and care of this pet. ________________

It is in account __________________ at ________________ (bank name)

located at ____________________________________ (bank address)

(contact name) at ________________ (phone number) can help you access these funds

❑ This pet is covered by pet insurance from __________________ (company name)

at ____ (address)

The policy number or identification number is ____________________________

Contact name: ________________ and telephone number: ________________

Pet Plans

❑ When this pet dies, if at all possible I would like his/her remains to be ______________________________

____

____

____

(Keep in mind that your wishes may not be possible, but you can at least explain your desires.)

____

❑ I would like this pet to participate in my funeral service as follows: ______________________________

____

____

(Be realistic here!)

Pet Preferences

Pet Name: ______________________________

Food at: (am and pm) ______________________________

Treats ______________________________

Toys ______________________________

Bed ______________________________

Kennel/Crate ______________________________

Commands ______________________________

Sleeps at night in the ______________________________

Pet Plans

I have the following pets. Instead of taking them to a shelter or selling them, I would like them to go to be handled as follows:

Pet's Name ____

Breed ________________________ Age __________________

Vet ________________________ Phone Number __________________

Medication ____

I'd like ______________________________ (name and phone number)

to care for this special pet because ______________________________

Health Concerns ____

This pet's personal items are located ______________________________

❑ I have set aside money for the maintenance and care of this pet. __________________

It is in account __________________ at __________________ (bank name)

located at __________________________________ (bank address)

(contact name) at __________________ (phone number) can help you access these funds

❑ This pet is covered by pet insurance from __________________ (company name)

at ____ (address)

The policy number or identification number is ______________________________

Contact name: __________________ and telephone number: __________________

CONTINUED

Pet Plans

☐ When this pet dies, if at all possible I would like his/her remains to be ______________________________

____

____

____

(Keep in mind that your wishes may not be possible, but you can at least explain your desires.)

____

☐ I would like this pet to participate in my funeral service as follows: ______________________

____

____

(Be realistic here!)

Pet Preferences

Pet Name: ____

Food at: (am and pm) ____

Treats ____

Toys ____

Bed ____

Kennel/Crate ____

Commands ____

Sleeps at night in the ____

Pets Who Have Passed

Previous Pet's Name: ____________________

Final Resting Place: ____________________

(Be sure to describe this completely.) ____________________

If there is a burial address and plot number or location, list it here: ____________________

____

❑ I would like this pet's cremated remains to join me in my final resting spot. (Remember, laws may govern here, but your request is at least worth sharing with your loved ones!) Be sure to explain this fully in the My Fabulous Funeral chapter!

____

____

Previous Pet's Name: ____________________

Final Resting Place: ____________________

(Be sure to describe this completely.) ____________________

If there is a burial address and plot number or location, list it here: ____________________

____

❑ I would like this pet's cremated remains to join me in my final resting spot. (Remember, laws may govern here, but your request is at least worth sharing with your loved ones!) Be sure to explain this fully in the My Fabulous Funeral chapter!Previous Pet's Name:

Final Resting Place: ____________________

(Be sure to describe this completely.) ____________________

Pets Who Have Passed

Previous Pet's Name: ______________________________

Final Resting Place: ______________________________

(Be sure to describe this completely.) ______________________________

If there is a burial address and plot number or location, list it here: ______________________________

____

❑ I would like this pet's cremated remains to join me in my final resting spot. (Remember, laws may govern here, but your request is at least worth sharing with your loved ones!) Be sure to explain this fully in the My Fabulous Funeral chapter!

____

____

Previous Pet's Name: ______________________________

Final Resting Place: ______________________________

(Be sure to describe this completely.) ______________________________

If there is a burial address and plot number or location, list it here: ______________________________

____

❑ I would like this pet's cremated remains to join me in my final resting spot. (Remember, laws may govern here, but your request is at least worth sharing with your loved ones!) Be sure to explain this fully in the My Fabulous Funeral chapter!Previous Pet's Name:

Final Resting Place: ______________________________

(Be sure to describe this completely.) ______________________________

Pets Who Have Passed

Previous Pet's Name: ____

Final Resting Place: ____

(Be sure to describe this completely.) ________________________________

If there is a burial address and plot number or location, list it here: ____________________

____

❑ I would like this pet's cremated remains to join me in my final resting spot. (Remember, laws may govern here, but your request is at least worth sharing with your loved ones!) Be sure to explain this fully in the My Fabulous Funeral chapter!

____

____

Previous Pet's Name: ____

Final Resting Place: ____

(Be sure to describe this completely.) ________________________________

If there is a burial address and plot number or location, list it here: ____________________

____

❑ I would like this pet's cremated remains to join me in my final resting spot. (Remember, laws may govern here, but your request is at least worth sharing with your loved ones!) Be sure to explain this fully in the My Fabulous Funeral chapter!Previous Pet's Name:

Final Resting Place: ____

(Be sure to describe this completely.) ________________________________

Pets Who Have Passed

Previous Pet's Name: ______________________________

Final Resting Place: ______________________________

(Be sure to describe this completely.) ______________________________

If there is a burial address and plot number or location, list it here: ______________________________

____

❑ I would like this pet's cremated remains to join me in my final resting spot. (Remember, laws may govern here, but your request is at least worth sharing with your loved ones!) Be sure to explain this fully in the My Fabulous Funeral chapter!

____

____

Previous Pet's Name: ______________________________

Final Resting Place: ______________________________

(Be sure to describe this completely.) ______________________________

If there is a burial address and plot number or location, list it here: ______________________________

____

❑ I would like this pet's cremated remains to join me in my final resting spot. (Remember, laws may govern here, but your request is at least worth sharing with your loved ones!) Be sure to explain this fully in the My Fabulous Funeral chapter!Previous Pet's Name:

Final Resting Place: ______________________________

(Be sure to describe this completely.) ______________________________

PART TWO

The Business Side of My Life

Where there's a will, I want to be in it."

Bumper Sticker

CHAPTER

5

Wills and Important Legal Stuff

This book is not a legal document. It is not a will or a trust. If you want to reduce paying estate taxes to Uncle Sam, consult an attorney or a financial planner who specializes in maximizing savings.

An attorney can draft your will. Some of the chapters in this book could provide good information for your will.

Wills and Important Legal Stuff

Five Tips about Legal Stuff:

1. Dying without a will is not a good idea. It is expensive for your heirs, plus you miss out on the opportunity to decide who gets your assets! (It is decided by law.)
2. See the American Bar Association website at www.findlegalhelp.org where you can click on your state to find a lawyer.
3. Determine your own destiny! If you do not properly (legally) determine how you want things handled, the court system will step in and do what they think is right based on rules and statutes. It is good to have the court system in place if we somehow fail to properly execute our directions, but it feels so much better to create your own destiny.
4. Update your will regularly.
5. File a copy of your will with your lawyer. Put an identical copy in another safe place. Feel free to give copies to appropriate family and friends.

Legal Documents

An Overview With Simple Definitions

There are five primary types of legal documents that are routinely drafted with the "end of life" in mind. The first two deal with ASSETS. Numbers 3 and 4 deal with HEALTH. The fifth is for the safe transfer of POWER while you are still in control and can identify the best person to handle business for you in case you cannot.

1. **Will** (The document most people are familiar with.)
   This document gives a legal disposition of assets, and must be "probated" or approved by the court.

2. **Living or Revocable Trust** This document is also used for the disposition of assets. The purpose behind a Living or Revocable Trust is to speed-up asset transfer (probating a will takes more time) and to reduce taxes. If you have one of these, your assets must be held in the name of the trust before you die for it to "work." Your bank account, houses, cars… anything with a title can be transferred upon your death without going to court if it is titled in your Living Trust. Anything not held in living trust will go to probate with or without a will.

3. **Living Will** (Also called a **Health Care Directive**, which is a much better term!) The term Living Will is really confusing. It is not a "will" in the sense of directing where my assets (my favorite chair, my car, etc.) should go. Rather, it is a document that says how I'd like my body treated while I'm living if I can't make decisions for myself. (That is why the term Health Care Directive is so much better!)

4. **A POLST** form (Physicians Orders for Life Sustaining Treatment) complements the Health Care Directive. It is a voluntary form designed for seriously ill or frail patients when such decisions may need to be made in a relatively short period of time.

5. **Power of Attorney** In a Power of Attorney document, you name the person who can act on your behalf when you can't act. You can set limits. For example, you can create a Durable Power of Attorney for Health Care and Durable Power of Attorney for Finances.

   Durable Power of Attorney for Health Care is used when you want to name someone to make decisions about your health if and when you cannot make those decisions. It is "durable" because it can be changed. If you get better/recover, and are able to make your own decisions, you can!

Legal Documents

Durable Power of Attorney for Finances is used when you want to name someone to make decisions about your finances and when you cannot make those decisions. Again, it is "durable" because it can be changed. If you are able to make financial decisions again, you can!

Probate – The word is used for the entire court-supervised process of managing and settling estates of dead people. That includes people who die without wills. The probate process involves publishing notices and court hearings. Fees are set by statute and/or the court (depending on state law) for attorneys, executors and administrators. There can be delays while waiting for creditors to file claims and for determining whether money was owed or not. Another important function of probate is to provide for the collection of any taxes due by reason of the deceased's death or on the transfer of his or her property.

Don't be scared to start this process. You can always change your will.

The first step in the probate process is to determine whether there is a will and then if the will is valid. The will must be filed with the appropriate court in the county where the deceased person lived, together with a petition to have the court approve the will and appoint the named executor. (The executor manages all the "business" that has to do with probating the will.) If there is no executor named (or if there is no will), the court will appoint an administrator.

"Avoiding" Probate

Some of the ways people take action to "avoid" probate include: Executing a Trust (and transferring possessions into the trust), making lifetime gifts, or putting all substantial property in joint tenancy with an automatic right of survivorship in the joint owner. The assets properly covered by those processes are excluded from probate. (Get legal advice here.)

Legal Documents for My Stuff

(and for care of any minor children)

To deal with my assets (my stuff) and my children, I (have or do not have) a:

Will ❑ Yes ❑ No **Living or Revocable Trust** ❑ Yes ❑ No

My original will is located in ______________________________

It was drafted by ______________________________

Contact Phone Number ______________________________

The executor of my will is ______________________________

My Living or Revocable Trust Agreement is located ______________________________

It was drafted by ______________________________

Contact phone number ______________________________

Legal Documents for My Care

To deal with my health in case I am incapacitated,

I ❑ have or ❑ do not have a **Living Will or Health Care Directive**.

My Living Will/Health Care Directive is located ______________________________

Contact name and phone number ______________________________

To guide my physicians

I ❑ have or ❑ do not have a **POLST**.

My **POLST** is located ______________________________

Contact name and phone number ______________________________

Legal Documents for My Care

I have executed the following Power of Attorney documents:

________________________________ date ________________

________________________________ date ________________

They can be found: ________________________________

Some Tips About Wills and Assets

Will Websites

We found www.suzeormanwillandtrust.com, www.legacywriter.com, www.nolo.com or www.legalzoom.com to name a few. We can't and don't recommend any specific ones. Just know that there are rules for all this "legal junk" by state. The documents often need to be signed and witnessed by two people (who aren't beneficiaries). A notary is highly recommended (and usually required).

Attorneys are able to draft more complex estate documents. Updates are usually less expensive than the initial estate documents, unless you have changed everything (or inflation has hit).

Storing Your Will

Only you can decide where to keep your estate documents. It is best to file a copy with your lawyer. Take the following into account in making your decision about where to store the original:

If you store it in a locked box, someone will need to have access to the box. That includes a bank safe deposit box. Safe deposit boxes can (in some states) be sealed upon death. Other states require a representative of the government to be present if the holder is deceased. If your will is locked inside, your loved ones could experience significant delays and difficulties.

If you keep it at home (unlocked), it could be lost or shredded, or it could burn in a fire. A small fireproof safe is best. Just make a note of the combination or key location.

Notes

"I don't believe in dying.
It's been done.
I'm working on a new
exit. Besides, I can't die
now. – I'm booked.
I can't afford to die. I'd
lose too much money."

George Burns

CHAPTER

6

Money In

This is where you write down
the money you receive.

Three Tips about Money In:

1. Try to make your Money In exceed your Money Out! (Don't use the Government for an example here.)
2. See if you can find some more money! Go to the unclaimed property websites to see if someone left you property that has been unclaimed! http://www.unclaimed.org/ and www.missingmoney.com
3. To appraise your business, to www.go-iba.org (Institute of Business Appraisers)

Financial Advisor

Name ____

Address ____

____

Phone Number ____________________________________

Accountant

Name ____

Address ____

____

Phone Number ____________________________________

Money I Receive

Paycheck from ______________________________

❑ each month or ❑ every two weeks in the amount of ______________

They mail it to the following address: ______________________

____

____

Alimony from ______________________________

❑ each month or ❑ every two weeks in the amount of ______________

They mail it to the following address: ______________________

____

____

Child Support from ______________________________

❑ each month or ❑ every two weeks in the amount of ______________

They mail it to the following address: ______________________

____

____

____

____

____

Money I Receive

The following items all ask for the name of the "beneficiary upon my death." Be careful to write the ACTUAL beneficiary who is listed on the legal paperwork, not just who you "wish" the beneficiary to be today.

____

Disability check each month in the amount of ______________________

They mail it to the following address ______________________

____

Beneficiary upon my death ______________________

____

Social Security check each month in the amount of ______________________

They mail it to the following address ______________________

____

Beneficiary upon my death ______________________

____

To report a death to The Social Security Administration, call 1-800 772-1213 between 7am and 7pm Eastern, Monday through Friday. They will ask you for the social security number of the deceased person. Hearing impaired TTY telephone number is 800-325-0778.

____

____

____

Money I Receive

Retirement or Pension check each month from ______________________________

in the amount of ______________________________

They mail it to the following address ______________________________

____

Beneficiary upon my death ______________________________

____

Retirement or Pension check each month from ______________________________

in the amount of ______________________________

They mail it to the following address ______________________________

____

Beneficiary upon my death ______________________________

____

Retirement or Pension check each month from ______________________________

in the amount of ______________________________

They mail it to the following address ______________________________

____

Beneficiary upon my death ______________________________

____

Money I Receive

Annuity check each month from ______________________________

in the amount of ______________________________

They mail it to the following address: ______________________________

____

Beneficiary upon my death: ______________________________

____

Annuity check each month from ______________________________

in the amount of ______________________________

They mail it to the following address: ______________________________

____

Beneficiary upon my death: ______________________________

____

Bond Revenue check each month from ______________________________

in the amount of ______________________________

They mail it to the following address: ______________________________

____

Beneficiary upon my death: ______________________________

____

Money I Receive

Other ____

check each month from ________________________________

in the amount of ___________________________________

They mail it to the following address: __________________________

____

Beneficiary upon my death: ________________________________

____

I own rental property located at ____________________ (city) ______ (state).

I receive rent in the amount of __________ on the ____________ day of the month from

____

Beneficiary upon my death: ________________________________

I own rental property located at ____________________ city ______ state

I receive rent in the amount of __________ on the ____________ day of the month from

____

Beneficiary upon my death ________________________________

____

____

____

Money I Receive

Someone owes me money.

Their name and address is ______________________________

____

and it was for ______________________________

The original amount is ______________ but they have been paying as follows

____

____

There is ❑ or is not ❑ a written document about this. It can be found in ______________

____

Someone else also owes me money.

Their name and address is ______________________________

____

and it was for ______________________________

The original amount is ______________ but they have been paying as follows

There is ❑ or is not ❑ a written document about this. It can be found in ______________

____

____

____

On-Line Financial Summary

With the advent of technology, there are now financial or economic modeling and monitoring websites. Participants can log all of their financial information into their personal, private database, and the systems monitor the performance of the investments. They can even make investment recommendations based on the information and goals you input.

If you have utilized one of these sites, it could help your loved ones if they had access to the site to ensure that they have accounted for all your assets.

I ❑ have subscribed to a financial/economic modeling website. The name of the website is:

www. ____

I ❑ have not subscribed to or utilized a financial/economic modeling website.

Bank Accounts and Investments

Tip: You may want to ask your financial advisor and/or attorney whether any of your stocks, bonds, or brokerage accounts would qualify under the Uniform Transfer on Death Security Registration Act, which allows for the transfer of those items without probate. You will need to fill out a beneficiary form, and comply with other requirements. While you are living, the beneficiary has no rights to the account, but when you die they have full ownership rights. (These are regulated by state, and can work for securities, real estate, automobiles and other assets. Check with your attorney to see what your options are, and to ensure that you properly execute documents to achieve your goals.) When you die, the beneficiary shows their ID and a death certificate to claim assets without going through probate.

Find my latest tax return, which is located in ______________________ to see if any other investments beyond those I have listed.

My accountant is: ______________________

CHECKING ACCOUNTS

Name of financial institution ______________________

Address ______________________ (city) __________ (state)

Account number ______________________

Name(s) on account ______________________

Phone Number: ______________________

Advisor's or Contact's Name: ______________________

ATM Card Number ______________________

____

____

Bank Accounts and Investments

CHECKING ACCOUNTS - CONTINUED

Name of financial institution ______________________________

Address ______________________________ (city) __________ (state)

Account number ______________________________

Name(s) on account ______________________________

Phone Number ______________________________

Advisor's or Contact's Name ______________________________

____

ATM Card Number ______________________________

Name of financial institution ______________________________

Address ______________________________ (city) __________ (state)

Account number ______________________________

Name(s) on account ______________________________

Phone Number ______________________________

Advisor's or Contact's Name ______________________________

ATM Card Number ______________________________

My checkbook is on Quickbooks or on ______________________________

You can find it on my ______________________________ (describe the computer).

Bank Accounts and Investments

SAVINGS ACCOUNTS

Name of financial institution ______________________________

Address ______________________________ (city) __________ (state)

Account number ______________________________

Name(s) on account ______________________________

Phone Number ______________________ Advisor's or Contact's Name ______________________

Name of financial institution ______________________________

Address ______________________________ (city) __________ (state)

Account number ______________________________

Name(s) on account ______________________________

Phone Number ______________________ Advisor's or Contact's Name ______________________

HOME EQUITY LINE OF CREDIT (HELOC)

Name of financial institution ______________________________

Address ______________________________ (city) __________ (state)

Account number ______________________________

Name(s) on account ______________________________

Phone Number ______________________ Advisor's or Contact's Name ______________________

Bank Accounts and Investments

CREDIT UNION ACCOUNTS

Name of financial institution ____________________

Address ____________________ (city) __________ (state)

Account number ____________________

Name(s) on account ____________________

Phone Number ____________________

Advisor's or Contact's Name ____________________

Name of financial institution ____________________

Address ____________________ (city) __________ (state)

Account number ____________________

Name(s) on account ____________________

Phone Number ____________________

Advisor's or Contact's Name ____________________

Bank Accounts and Investments

IRAs

Name of financial institution ____________________

Address ____________________ (city) __________ (state)

Account number ____________________

Name(s) on account ____________________

Phone Number ____________________

Advisor's or Contact's Name ____________________

Name of financial institution ____________________

Address ____________________ (city) __________ (state)

Account number ____________________

Name(s) on account ____________________

Phone Number ____________________

Advisor's or Contact's Name ____________________

Bank Accounts and Investments

KEOGH PLANS

Name of financial institution ______________________

Address ______________________ (city) __________ (state)

Account number ______________________

Name(s) on account ______________________

Phone Number ______________________

Advisor's or Contact's Name ______________________

Name of financial institution ______________________

Address ______________________ (city) __________ (state)

Account number ______________________

Name(s) on account ______________________

Phone Number ______________________

Advisor's or Contact's Name ______________________

Bank Accounts and Investments

SEP IRAs

Name of financial institution ______________________________

Address ______________________________ (city) __________ (state)

Account number ______________________________

Name(s) on account ______________________________

Phone Number ______________________________

Advisor's or Contact's Name ______________________________

Name of financial institution ______________________________

Address ______________________________ (city) __________ (state)

Account number ______________________________

Name(s) on account ______________________________

Phone Number ______________________________

Advisor's or Contact's Name ______________________________

Bank Accounts and Investments

ROTH IRAs

Name of financial institution ______________________________

Address ______________________________ (city) __________ (state)

Account number ______________________________

Name(s) on account ______________________________

Phone Number ______________________________

Advisor's or Contact's Name ______________________________

Name of financial institution ______________________________

Address ______________________________ (city) __________ (state)

Account number ______________________________

Name(s) on account ______________________________

Phone Number ______________________________

Advisor's or Contact's Name ______________________________

Bank Accounts and Investments

401Ks and Single Ks

Name of financial institution ______________________________

Address ______________________________ (city) __________ (state)

Account number ______________________________

Name(s) on account ______________________________

Phone Number ______________________________

Advisor's or Contact's Name ______________________________

Name of financial institution ______________________________

Address ______________________________ (city) __________ (state)

Account number ______________________________

Name(s) on account ______________________________

Phone Number ______________________________

Advisor's or Contact's Name ______________________________

Name of financial institution ______________________________

Address ______________________________ (city) __________ (state)

Account number ______________________________

Name(s) on account ______________________________

Phone Number ______________________________

Advisor's or Contact's Name ______________________________

Bank Accounts and Investments

STOCKS

Individual Stocks I hold (not in mutual funds, etc.)

Name of Stock	Call Letters	Number of Shares	Certificates are located in:

Bank Accounts and Investments

MUTUAL FUNDS

Name of Fund	Call Letters	Number of Shares	Paperwork located in:

Bank Accounts and Investments

ANNUITIES

Broker Name	Annuity Name	Contact Number	Contract Beginning and Ending Date

Bank Accounts and Investments

BONDS

Name of Bond	Rate	Maturity Date	Bonds are located in:

GOLD BRICKS, PRECIOUS METALS AND GEMS

Located in	Quantity or description

Bank Accounts and Investments

CD's

Institution	Date of Origin	Date at Maturity	CDs are located in:

OTHER ACCOUNTS

Name of financial institution ______________________________

Address ______________________________ city ____________ state

Account number ______________ Phone Number ______________

Advisor's or Contact's Name ______________________________

Name on account ______________________________

Businesses I Own or Have Owned

Name of Business: ______________________________

Type (Sole Proprietorship, Corporation or Partnership) ______________________________

Percentage Ownership ______________________________

Other Owners ______________________________

____

Attorney with knowledge of business: ______________________________

Phone number of attorney: ______________________________

Why this business matters to me, and why I started or invested in it: ______________________________

____

____

____

____

____

❑ Currently own OR ______________________________

❑ Sold on ____________ and currently receive $ ____________ as a result of the sale

____

____

____

Businesses I Own or Have Owned

Name of Business: ______________________________

Type (Sole Proprietorship, Corporation or Partnership) ______________________________

Percentage Ownership ______________________________

Other Owners ______________________________

____

Attorney with knowledge of business: ______________________________

Phone number of attorney: ______________________________

Why this business matters to me, and why I started or invested in it ______________________________

____

____

____

____

____

❑ Currently own OR ______________________________

❑ Sold on ____________ and currently receive $ ____________ as a result of the sale

____

____

____

Businesses I Own or Have Owned

Name of Business: ____

Type (Sole Proprietorship, Corporation or Partnership) ________________________

Percentage Ownership ______________________________________

Other Owners ____

____

Attorney with knowledge of business: ________________________________

Phone number of attorney: ______________________________________

Why this business matters to me, and why I started or invested in it: ________________

____

____

____

____

____

❑ Currently own OR ____

❑ Sold on ______________ and currently receive $ ______________ as a result of the sale

____

____

____

Businesses I Own or Have Owned

Name of Business: ______________________________

Type (Sole Proprietorship, Corporation or Partnership) ______________________________

Percentage Ownership ______________________________

Other Owners ______________________________

____

Attorney with knowledge of business: ______________________________

Phone number of attorney: ______________________________

Why this business matters to me, and why I started or invested in it: ______________________________

____

____

____

____

____

❑ Currently own OR ______________________________

❑ Sold on ____________ and currently receive $ ____________ as a result of the sale

____

____

____

"In this world nothing is certain but death and taxes."

Benjamin Franklin

CHAPTER

7

Money Out

This is where you list the ways you spend money.

Two Tips about Money Out:

1. Keep track of your money spent, and actively manage it!
2. Sites like www.simpleplanning.com, www.mint.com, and www.quicken.com offer tracking mechanisms.
3. Search *Checkbook* in the App Store.

We do not recommend any, we just say they are out there.

House and Car Payments

Rent for ______________________________ (address)

in the amount of ______________ is due on the ______________ (date) of each month

House Payment for ______________________________ (address)

in the amount of ______________ is due on the ______________ (date) of each month

House Payment for ______________________________ (address)

in the amount of ______________ is due on the ______________ (date) of each month

Car Payments ______________________________

Car Name ______________ Institution ______________ Account ______________

Monthly Payment ______________ Projected Final Payment Date: ______________

Car Name ______________ Institution ______________ Account ______________

Monthly Payment ______________ Projected Final Payment Date: ______________

Car Name ______________ Institution ______________ Account ______________

Monthly Payment ______________ Projected Final Payment Date: ______________

Other Vehicle Payments ______________________________

Vehicle Name ______________ Institution ______________ Account ______________

Monthly Payment ______________ Projected Final Payment Date: ______________

____

____

Credit Cards

Card Type Visa/MC/Am Express/Discover/ Store Name	Bank Name	Card Number

Living Expenses

Expense **Approximate Amount**

Alarm Company ______________________________

Auto Insurance ______________________________

Cable/Satellite ______________________________

Cell Phone ______________________________

Club(s) ______________________________

____

Disability Insurance ______________________________

Electric ______________________________

Gas ______________________________

Health Insurance ______________________________

Home Owner's Insurance ______________________________

House Phone ______________________________

Internet ______________________________

Lawn Care ______________________________

Life Insurance ______________________________

____

____

Living Expenses

(CONTINUED)

Expense	Approximate Amount
Magazine(s)	
Newspaper(s)	
Safety Deposit Box	
Storage	
Sewer	
Trash	
Water	
Doctor and Hospital Bills	

Special Gifts and Endowments

I have a fund at the ______________________________ Community Foundation.

Contact name and number ______________________________

I currently make donations to the following charities: ______________________________

____

____

____

____

I ❑ have or ❑ would like to set up an endowment to benefit. (explain).

____

____

____

____

____

____

____

____

I'm remembering my sorority, Kappa Kappa Gamma, in my Will with an estate gift. Don't forget your favorite organization.

"Where does stuff go when it dies, does it go to stuff heaven?"

George Carlin

CHAPTER

8

All My Stuff

Your stuff is valuable. This is where you tell all about it.

Resources and Tips About "Stuff"

1. Consider photographing your "especially valuable" ($$) stuff, or the items you cherish most. That way your loved ones will know what they are looking for.

2. You can get information about appraisals and find an appraiser for your valuables from the American Society of Appraisers at www.appraisers.org, telephone number 800-ASA-VALU.

3. If you have unique items and want information about their value generally, go to websites like www.antiques.about.com and www.westercollectables.net. Basically, just research things you think may be valuable and keep documentation in a file so your loved ones won't have to figure it out on their own.

4. Antiques Road Show, on PBS often has surprising information. Their website, www.pbs.org/wgbh/roadshow is not only fun to browse, but can also be a great resource. You may have a treasure!

Approximately How Valuable is My Stuff?

Be sure to have your valuable stuff appraised if you are concerned about dividing your estate among your heirs. If you have any concern about theft or loss of any kind, you should also look into obtaining insurance for the item or items.

If you obtain appraisals now (as you look at your estate before you die), they can help in four ways:

1. You will know the value of your estate as of the date(s) of the appraisals. (Be aware, though, that values are determined as of the date of death.)

2. Your attorney or financial advisor may review the appraisals to determine what types of legal documents make the most sense for estate planning purposes.

3. The documentation can serve as a starting point for your loved ones so they know which valuables they should look for upon your death. Appraisals with photos will remove questions about "what" the object looks like. The valuable pearl necklace is the one that looks like xyz, as opposed to the one that looks like abc, for example.

4. Appraisals can help for insurance purposes now, while you are alive. If you find items of particular value, be sure to discuss insuring them. You may elect not to, but at least you will make an informed decision.

5. Consider an additional "rider" on your home owner's policy for the most valuable items.

I was convinced to sell my great-great-aunt Peggy's doggie doorstop in a garage sale for $20 because it didn't fit our décor. I saw one (maybe the same one) in a store a few years later for just under $600. DARN! – I felt both an emotional and financial loss!

Consider having your valuables appraised every 10 years or so – especially those of "high" value. Keep the appraisals locked in a safe place that your loved ones can access! Of course, also consider insuring them.

Dividing Your Stuff – Some Thoughts

There are three general ways to divide estates, but the BEST way will probably take into consideration or implement portions of each of the following concepts. Your estate and your relationships with people you love are a unique matter!

1. Specify that your estate be divided by certain percentages upon your death. The trouble here can be that certain people may not receive specific cherished items.

2. Assign specific items to specific people without regard to comparative dollar value at the time of your death. (Be aware that there could be hurt feelings in the future if some items left to some people end up being worth vastly more than other items.)

3. Assign specific items to specific people based on today's market values. If you are trying to divide your estate based on today's market value, you need to keep your eyes on any changes in relative worth since valuables are assigned a dollar value typically as of the date of death. As with everything, there could be some exceptions based on governing laws.

Explain the reasons you are giving certain people certain items. The warm thoughts may matter more than the stuff!

Hide and Seek, Find My Hidden Stuff!

I have some special things hidden in these places:

____

____

____

____

____

____

____

____

____

____

____

____

____

____

____

____

____

____

Do you hide things under the mattress, buried, in a coffee can, in the attic, in a drawer, in a fake book, or in the refrigerator or freezer? How about cash in the bottom of curtains or in a band-aid box? Maybe something special is in the attic eaves? These are all real places we have seen stuff hidden! Be sure to tell your loved ones to look in your secret hiding places or things you find dear may be overlooked.

Make sure the people you want to inherit your stuff can FIND your stuff! Places like the "Spy Museum" sell fake food containers that weigh what you'd expect them to weigh. Great places to hide valuables . . . unless someone unknowingly tosses them in the trash!

Stuff in Storage

Wall safe located ______________________________

name) at ______________________________(phone number)

has the combination, or the keys are located ______________________________

____

Movable safe located ______________________________

(name) at ______________________________(phone number)

has the combination, or the keys are located ______________________________

____

Other container/storage ______________________________(description) located

(name) at ______________________________(phone number)

______________________________has the access information or opening instructions

Other container/storage ______________________________(description) located

(name) at ______________________________(phone number)

______________________________has the access information or opening instructions

Other container/storage ______________________________(description) located

(name) at ______________________________(phone number)

______________________________has the access information or opening instructions

____

Stuff in Storage

I have stored valuables in the following locations:

Safe deposit box located at ________________ bank at ________________________________ (address)

The key for the box is located ____

____

Safe deposit box located at ________________ bank at ________________________________ (address)

The key for the box is located ____

____

Storage unit with ____ (storage company name)

located at ____ (address)

The keys are located __________________________________ or the combination is _________________

____

Storage unit with ____ (storage company name)

located at ____ (address)

The keys are located __________________________________ or the combination is _________________

____

Gun safe located _________________ (name) at ______________ (phone number) has the combination

or the keys are located ____

____

Art

PIECE NAME ____

Description____

Artist's name ________________________ date completed ________

Date acquired______________ acquisition cost __________________

Current location ____________________________(where you can find it)

Appraisal by____________ on _________(date) located: ____________

Desired beneficiary/beneficiaries: ______________________________

and why____

____

❑ Your name is written on the back._________________

Is it a treasure? If so, explain (dollar or sentimental value):

____

____

____

❑ I have included a photograph of this piece.______________

____

____

____

Some of the detail on this page and the following pages can make a big difference to your loved ones, either emotionally or financially! Have you ever seen American Pickers on TV? A little history can make a big difference.

Art

PIECE NAME ______________________________

Description ______________________________

Artist's name ______________________ date completed __________

Date acquired ______________ acquisition cost ______________

Current location ______________________ (where you can find it)

Appraisal by ____________ on __________ (date) located: __________

Desired beneficiary/beneficiaries: ______________________

and why ______________________________

____

☐ Your name is written on the back. ______________________

Is it a treasure? If so, explain (dollar or sentimental value): ______________

____

____

____

☐ I have included a photograph of this piece. ______________

____

____

____

Art

PIECE NAME ____

Description ____

Artist's name ______________________________ date completed ______________

Date acquired ____________________ acquisition cost ______________________

Current location ____________________________________ (where you can find it)

Appraisal by ________________ on ____________ (date) located: ______________

Desired beneficiary/beneficiaries: ______________________________________

and why ____

____

❑ Your name is written on the back. _____________________________________

Is it a treasure? If so, explain (dollar or sentimental value): _______________

____

____

____

❑ I have included a photograph of this piece. ___________________________

____

____

____

Art

PIECE NAME ____________________

Description ____________________

Artist's name ____________________ date completed ____________________

Date acquired ____________________ acquisition cost ____________________

Current location ____________________ (where you can find it)

Appraisal by ____________________ on ____________________ (date) located: ____________________

Desired beneficiary/beneficiaries: ____________________

and why ____________________

____

❑ Your name is written on the back. ____________________

Is it a treasure? If so, explain (dollar or sentimental value): ____________________

____

____

____

❑ I have included a photograph of this piece. ____________________

____

____

____

Art

PIECE NAME ____________________

Description ____________________

Artist's name ____________________ date completed ____________________

Date acquired ____________________ acquisition cost ____________________

Current location ____________________ (where you can find it)

Appraisal by ____________________ on ____________________ (date) located: ____________________

Desired beneficiary/beneficiaries: ____________________

and why ____________________

____

❑ Your name is written on the back. ____________________

Is it a treasure? If so, explain (dollar or sentimental value): ____________________

____

____

____

❑ I have included a photograph of this piece. ____________________

____

____

____

Art

PIECE NAME ______________________________

Description______________________________

Artist's name ______________________ date completed ____________

Date acquired________________ acquisition cost ________________

Current location ______________________(where you can find it)

Appraisal by____________ on ____________(date) located: ____________

Desired beneficiary/beneficiaries: ______________________

and why______________________________

____

❑ Your name is written on the back. ______________________

Is it a treasure? If so, explain (dollar or sentimental value): ____________

____

____

____

❑ I have included a photograph of this piece.______________________

____

____

____

Art

PIECE NAME ____

Description____

Artist's name ________________________ date completed __________

Date acquired________________ acquisition cost __________________

Current location ____________________________(where you can find it)

Appraisal by____________ on __________(date) located: ____________

Desired beneficiary/beneficiaries: ______________________________

and why____

____

❑ Your name is written on the back. ______________________________

Is it a treasure? If so, explain (dollar or sentimental value): ____________________

____

____

____

❑ I have included a photograph of this piece.__________________________

____

____

____

Art

PIECE NAME ______________________________

Description ______________________________

Artist's name ______________________ date completed ____________

Date acquired ______________ acquisition cost ______________

Current location ______________________ (where you can find it)

Appraisal by ____________ on __________ (date) located: __________

Desired beneficiary/beneficiaries: ______________________

and why ______________________________

____

❑ Your name is written on the back. ______________________

Is it a treasure? If so, explain (dollar or sentimental value): ______________

____

____

____

❑ I have included a photograph of this piece. ______________________

____

____

____

If you want your stuff to be distributed to specific people, the ONLY way to ensure they receive it is to specify your wishes in a properly executed legal document (will or trust). My grandmothers and great auntie all taped tiny pieces of paper with our names onto the items they wanted us to receive. My grandfather wrote our names in red grease pencil in his distinct handwriting on the back of furniture.

Tell the stories about how you acquired your stuff. People who love you will treasure your stuff if they understand WHY it is special to you!
My Grandmother left me some old china pieces… from China… and I wonder how she came to own them!

❑ **Coins** ❑ **Collectibles** ❑ **China** ❑ **Crystal** ❑ **Family Treasures**
❑ **Furniture** ❑ **Guns** ❑ **Jewelry** ❑ **Silver** ❑ **Other**

ITEM ______________________________

Description ______________________________

Brand name and make ______________________________

Date acquired ______________________________

for (e.g., wedding gift, anniversary gift, inherited from someone, etc.) ______________________________

____

____

and current location ______________________________ (where you can find it)

Appraisal by ______________________________

on ______________ (date) is located: ______________________________

Desired beneficiary/beneficiaries, and why ______________________________

____

____

Is it a treasure? If so, explain (dollar or sentimental value): ______________________________

____

____

❑ I have included a photograph of it. ______________________________

____

❑ **Coins** ❑ **Collectibles** ❑ **China** ❑ **Crystal** ❑ **Family Treasures**

❑ **Furniture** ❑ **Guns** ❑ **Jewelry** ❑ **Silver** ❑ **Other**

ITEM ____

Description ____

Brand name and make ____

Date acquired ____

for (e.g., wedding gift, anniversary gift, inherited from someone, etc.) ______________________

____

____

and current location ______________________________ (where you can find it)

Appraisal by ____

on ______________ (date) is located: ______________________________

Desired beneficiary/beneficiaries, and why ______________________________

____

____

Is it a treasure? If so, explain (dollar or sentimental value): ______________________

____

____

❑ I have included a photograph of it. ______________________________

____

❑ **Coins** ❑ **Collectibles** ❑ **China** ❑ **Crystal** ❑ **Family Treasures**
❑ **Furniture** ❑ **Guns** ❑ **Jewelry** ❑ **Silver** ❑ **Other**

ITEM ____

Description ____

Brand name and make ____

Date acquired ____

for (e.g., wedding gift, anniversary gift, inherited from someone, etc.) ______________________

____

____

and current location ______________________________ (where you can find it)

Appraisal by ____

on ______________ (date) is located: ______________________

Desired beneficiary/beneficiaries, and why ______________________

____

____

Is it a treasure? If so, explain (dollar or sentimental value): ______________

____

____

❑ I have included a photograph of it. ______________________

____

I have left instructions to return my sorority pin to the Kappa Kappa Gamma Headquarters. Be specific about such items you have enjoyed too.

❑ **Coins** ❑ **Collectibles** ❑ **China** ❑ **Crystal** ❑ **Family Treasures**
❑ **Furniture** ❑ **Guns** ❑ **Jewelry** ❑ **Silver** ❑ **Other**

ITEM ____

Description ____

Brand name and make ____

Date acquired ____

for (e.g., wedding gift, anniversary gift, inherited from someone, etc.) ______________________________

____

____

and current location ______________________________ (where you can find it)

Appraisal by ____

on ______________ (date) is located: ______________________________

Desired beneficiary/beneficiaries, and why ______________________________

____

____

Is it a treasure? If so, explain (dollar or sentimental value): ______________________

____

____

❑ I have included a photograph of it. ______________________________

____

❑ **Coins** ❑ **Collectibles** ❑ **China** ❑ **Crystal** ❑ **Family Treasures**
❑ **Furniture** ❑ **Guns** ❑ **Jewelry** ❑ **Silver** ❑ **Other**

ITEM ____

Description ____

Brand name and make ____

Date acquired ____

for (e.g., wedding gift, anniversary gift, inherited from someone, etc.) ______________________

____

____

and current location ______________________________ (where you can find it)

Appraisal by ____

on ______________(date) is located: ______________________________

Desired beneficiary/beneficiaries, and why ______________________________

____

____

Is it a treasure? If so, explain (dollar or sentimental value): ______________________

____

____

❑ I have included a photograph of it. ______________________________

____

❑ **Coins** ❑ **Collectibles** ❑ **China** ❑ **Crystal** ❑ **Family Treasures**
❑ **Furniture** ❑ **Guns** ❑ **Jewelry** ❑ **Silver** ❑ **Other**

ITEM ____

Description ____

Brand name and make ____

Date acquired ____

for (e.g., wedding gift, anniversary gift, inherited from someone, etc.) ____________________

____

____

and current location ______________________________ (where you can find it)

Appraisal by ____

on ______________ (date) is located: ______________________________

Desired beneficiary/beneficiaries, and why ______________________________

____

____

Is it a treasure? If so, explain (dollar or sentimental value): ______________

____

____

❑ I have included a photograph of it. ______________

____

Coins can be very valuable. Be sure to handle them with respect.

❑ **Coins** ❑ **Collectibles** ❑ **China** ❑ **Crystal** ❑ **Family Treasures**
❑ **Furniture** ❑ **Guns** ❑ **Jewelry** ❑ **Silver** ❑ **Other**

ITEM ____________________

Description ____________________

Brand name and make ____________________

Date acquired ____________________

for (e.g., wedding gift, anniversary gift, inherited from someone, etc.) ____________________

____

____

and current location ____________________ (where you can find it)

Appraisal by ____________________

on ____________ (date) is located: ____________________

Desired beneficiary/beneficiaries, and why ____________________

____

____

Is it a treasure? If so, explain (dollar or sentimental value): ____________________

____

____

❑ I have included a photograph of it. ____________________

____

❑ Coins ❑ Collectibles ❑ China ❑ Crystal ❑ Family Treasures
❑ Furniture ❑ Guns ❑ Jewelry ❑ Silver ❑ Other

ITEM ______________________________

Description ______________________________

Brand name and make ______________________________

Date acquired ______________________________

for (e.g., wedding gift, anniversary gift, inherited from someone, etc.) ______________________________

____

____

and current location ______________________________ (where you can find it)

Appraisal by ______________________________

on ______________ (date) is located: ______________________________

Desired beneficiary/beneficiaries, and why ______________________________

____

____

Is it a treasure? If so, explain (dollar or sentimental value): ______________________________

____

____

❑ I have included a photograph of it. ______________________________

____

Think about ornaments, autographed books, dolls, and antique toys. I have a Steinbach Nutcracker collection. It belongs right here on this page!

❑ **Coins** ❑ **Collectibles** ❑ **China** ❑ **Crystal** ❑ **Family Treasures**
❑ **Furniture** ❑ **Guns** ❑ **Jewelry** ❑ **Silver** ❑ **Other**

ITEM ______________________________

Description ______________________________

Brand name and make ______________________________

Date acquired ______________________________

for (e.g., wedding gift, anniversary gift, inherited from someone, etc.) ______________________________

____

____

and current location ______________________________ (where you can find it)

Appraisal by ______________________________

on ______________ (date) is located: ______________________________

Desired beneficiary/beneficiaries, and why ______________________________

____

____

Is it a treasure? If so, explain (dollar or sentimental value): ______________________________

____

____

❑ I have included a photograph of it. ______________________________

____

❑ **Coins** ❑ **Collectibles** ❑ **China** ❑ **Crystal** ❑ **Family Treasures**
❑ **Furniture** ❑ **Guns** ❑ **Jewelry** ❑ **Silver** ❑ **Other**

ITEM ____

Description ____

Brand name and make ____

Date acquired ____

for (e.g., wedding gift, anniversary gift, inherited from someone, etc.) ____________________

____

____

and current location ______________________________ (where you can find it)

Appraisal by ____

on ____________ (date) is located: ______________________________

Desired beneficiary/beneficiaries, and why ______________________________

____

____

Is it a treasure? If so, explain (dollar or sentimental value): ____________________

____

____

❑ I have included a photograph of it. ______________________________

____

❑ **Coins** ❑ **Collectibles** ❑ **China** ❑ **Crystal** ❑ **Family Treasures**
❑ **Furniture** ❑ **Guns** ❑ **Jewelry** ❑ **Silver** ❑ **Other**

ITEM ____

Description ____

Brand name and make ____

Date acquired ____

for (e.g., wedding gift, anniversary gift, inherited from someone, etc.) ____________________

____

____

and current location ____________________ (where you can find it)

Appraisal by ____

on ______________ (date) is located: ____________________

Desired beneficiary/beneficiaries, and why ____________________

____

____

Is it a treasure? If so, explain (dollar or sentimental value): ______________

____

____

❑ I have included a photograph of it. ____________________

____

Don't forget antique tools and sports memorabilia! My grandpa was a carpenter and had some amazing antique tools! One of my good friends has hundreds of baseballs and baseball cards! I'll bet there are some real gems in that collection!

❑ **Coins** ❑ **Collectibles** ❑ **China** ❑ **Crystal** ❑ **Family Treasures**
❑ **Furniture** ❑ **Guns** ❑ **Jewelry** ❑ **Silver** ❑ **Other**

ITEM ____

Description ____

Brand name and make ____

Date acquired ____

for (e.g., wedding gift, anniversary gift, inherited from someone, etc.) ____________________

____

____

and current location ______________________________ (where you can find it)

Appraisal by ____

on ______________ (date) is located: ______________________________

Desired beneficiary/beneficiaries, and why ______________________________

____

____

Is it a treasure? If so, explain (dollar or sentimental value): ____________________

____

____

❑ I have included a photograph of it. ______________________________

____

❑ Coins ❑ Collectibles ❑ China ❑ Crystal ❑ Family Treasures
❑ Furniture ❑ Guns ❑ Jewelry ❑ Silver ❑ Other

ITEM ___

Description ___

Brand name and make ___

Date acquired ___

for (e.g., wedding gift, anniversary gift, inherited from someone, etc.) ___

___

___

and current location ___ (where you can find it)

Appraisal by ___

on ___ (date) is located: ___

Desired beneficiary/beneficiaries, and why ___

___

___

Is it a treasure? If so, explain (dollar or sentimental value): ___

___

___

❑ I have included a photograph of it. ___

___

My mom brought her crystal back from Europe on her only trip there. It's hand etched and very delicate. We seldom use it because it has so much sentimental value to me!

❑ **Coins** ❑ **Collectibles** ❑ **China** ❑ **Crystal** ❑ **Family Treasures**
❑ **Furniture** ❑ **Guns** ❑ **Jewelry** ❑ **Silver** ❑ **Other**

ITEM ____

Description ____

Brand name and make ____

Date acquired ____

for (e.g., wedding gift, anniversary gift, inherited from someone, etc.) ______________________

____

____

and current location ______________________________ (where you can find it)

Appraisal by ____

on ______________ (date) is located: ______________________________

Desired beneficiary/beneficiaries, and why ______________________________

____

____

Is it a treasure? If so, explain (dollar or sentimental value): ______________________

____

____

❑ I have included a photograph of it. ______________________________

____

❑ **Coins** ❑ **Collectibles** ❑ **China** ❑ **Crystal** ❑ **Family Treasures**
❑ **Furniture** ❑ **Guns** ❑ **Jewelry** ❑ **Silver** ❑ **Other**

ITEM ____

Description ____

Brand name and make ____

Date acquired ____

for (e.g., wedding gift, anniversary gift, inherited from someone, etc.) ______________________

____

____

and current location ______________________________ (where you can find it)

Appraisal by ____

on ______________ (date) is located: ______________________________

Desired beneficiary/beneficiaries, and why ______________________________

____

____

Is it a treasure? If so, explain (dollar or sentimental value): ______________________

____

____

❑ I have included a photograph of it. ______________________________

____

❑ **Coins** ❑ **Collectibles** ❑ **China** ❑ **Crystal** ❑ **Family Treasures**

❑ **Furniture** ❑ **Guns** ❑ **Jewelry** ❑ **Silver** ❑ **Other**

ITEM ______________________________

Description ______________________________

Brand name and make ______________________________

Date acquired ______________________________

for (e.g., wedding gift, anniversary gift, inherited from someone, etc.) ______________________________

____

____

and current location ______________________________ (where you can find it)

Appraisal by ______________________________

on ______________ (date) is located: ______________________________

Desired beneficiary/beneficiaries, and why ______________________________

____

____

Is it a treasure? If so, explain (dollar or sentimental value): ______________________________

____

____

❑ I have included a photograph of it. ______________________________

____

❑ **Coins** ❑ **Collectibles** ❑ **China** ❑ **Crystal** ❑ **Family Treasures**
❑ **Furniture** ❑ **Guns** ❑ **Jewelry** ❑ **Silver** ❑ **Other**

ITEM ____

Description ____

Brand name and make ____

Date acquired ____

for (e.g., wedding gift, anniversary gift, inherited from someone, etc.) ______________________

____

____

and current location ______________________________ (where you can find it)

Appraisal by ____

on ____________ (date) is located: ______________________________

Desired beneficiary/beneficiaries, and why ______________________________

____

____

Is it a treasure? If so, explain (dollar or sentimental value): ______________________

____

____

❑ I have included a photograph of it. ______________________________

____

❑ **Coins** ❑ **Collectibles** ❑ **China** ❑ **Crystal** ❑ **Family Treasures**
❑ **Furniture** ❑ **Guns** ❑ **Jewelry** ❑ **Silver** ❑ **Other**

ITEM ____

Description ____

Brand name and make ____

Date acquired ____

for (e.g., wedding gift, anniversary gift, inherited from someone, etc.) ____________________

____

____

and current location ______________________________ (where you can find it)

Appraisal by ____

on ______________ (date) is located: ______________________________

Desired beneficiary/beneficiaries, and why ______________________________

____

____

Is it a treasure? If so, explain (dollar or sentimental value): ____________________

____

____

❑ I have included a photograph of it. ______________________________

____

❑ **Coins** ❑ **Collectibles** ❑ **China** ❑ **Crystal** ❑ **Family Treasures**
❑ **Furniture** ❑ **Guns** ❑ **Jewelry** ❑ **Silver** ❑ **Other**

ITEM ______________________________

Description ______________________________

Brand name and make ______________________________

Date acquired ______________________________

for (e.g., wedding gift, anniversary gift, inherited from someone, etc.) ______________________________

____

____

and current location ______________________________ (where you can find it)

Appraisal by ______________________________

on ____________ (date) is located: ______________________________

Desired beneficiary/beneficiaries, and why ______________________________

____

____

Is it a treasure? If so, explain (dollar or sentimental value): ______________________________

____

____

❑ I have included a photograph of it. ______________________________

____

❑ **Coins** ❑ **Collectibles** ❑ **China** ❑ **Crystal** ❑ **Family Treasures**

❑ **Furniture** ❑ **Guns** ❑ **Jewelry** ❑ **Silver** ❑ **Other**

ITEM ____

Description ____

Brand name and make ____

Date acquired ____

for (e.g., wedding gift, anniversary gift, inherited from someone, etc.) ____________

____

____

and current location ____________________ (where you can find it)

Appraisal by ____

on ____________(date) is located: ______________________________

Desired beneficiary/beneficiaries, and why ______________________________

____

____

Is it a treasure? If so, explain (dollar or sentimental value): ____________

____

____

❑ I have included a photograph of it. ______________________________

____

My mom, who died way too young, embroidered the face of a clock. Her father, my granddaddy, made a frame for it and added electric arms. Her mom, my grandmother, taught me how to tell time on it when I was a little girl. I've upgraded it to batteries and hung it on a kitchen wall where I see it, and use it, all the time.

❑ Coins ❑ Collectibles ❑ China ❑ Crystal ❑ Family Treasures
❑ Furniture ❑ Guns ❑ Jewelry ❑ Silver ❑ Other

ITEM ____________________

Description ____________________

Brand name and make ____________________

Date acquired ____________________

for (e.g., wedding gift, anniversary gift, inherited from someone, etc.) ____________________

____

____

and current location ____________________ (where you can find it)

Appraisal by ____________________

on __________ (date) is located: ____________________

Desired beneficiary/beneficiaries, and why ____________________

____

____

Is it a treasure? If so, explain (dollar or sentimental value): ____________________

____

____

❑ I have included a photograph of it. ____________________

____

❑ **Coins** ❑ **Collectibles** ❑ **China** ❑ **Crystal** ❑ **Family Treasures**

❑ **Furniture** ❑ **Guns** ❑ **Jewelry** ❑ **Silver** ❑ **Other**

ITEM ____

Description ____

Brand name and make ____

Date acquired ____

for (e.g., wedding gift, anniversary gift, inherited from someone, etc.) ____

____

____

and current location ______________________________ (where you can find it)

Appraisal by ____

on ______________ (date) is located: ____

Desired beneficiary/beneficiaries, and why ____

____

____

Is it a treasure? If so, explain (dollar or sentimental value): ____

____

____

❑ I have included a photograph of it. ____

____

❑ **Coins** ❑ **Collectibles** ❑ **China** ❑ **Crystal** ❑ **Family Treasures**
❑ **Furniture** ❑ **Guns** ❑ **Jewelry** ❑ **Silver** ❑ **Other**

ITEM ____________________

Description ____________________

Brand name and make ____________________

Date acquired ____________________

for (e.g., wedding gift, anniversary gift, inherited from someone, etc.) ____________________

____

____

and current location ____________________ (where you can find it)

Appraisal by ____________________

on ____________ (date) is located: ____________________

Desired beneficiary/beneficiaries, and why ____________________

____

____

Is it a treasure? If so, explain (dollar or sentimental value): ____________________

____

____

❑ I have included a photograph of it. ____________________

____

My grandmother Chinnery gave me old, old, old photos when I was a teenager, well before she died. She just wanted me to have them. I dearly love the photos, and have written what she told me about them. This page is a great place to list information about special family photos!

❑ **Coins** ❑ **Collectibles** ❑ **China** ❑ **Crystal** ❑ **Family Treasures**
❑ **Furniture** ❑ **Guns** ❑ **Jewelry** ❑ **Silver** ❑ **Other**

ITEM ____

Description ____

Brand name and make ____

Date acquired ____

for (e.g., wedding gift, anniversary gift, inherited from someone, etc.) ____

____

____

and current location ____ (where you can find it)

Appraisal by ____

on ______________(date) is located: ____

Desired beneficiary/beneficiaries, and why ____

____

____

Is it a treasure? If so, explain (dollar or sentimental value): ____

____

____

❑ I have included a photograph of it. ____

____

❑ **Coins** ❑ **Collectibles** ❑ **China** ❑ **Crystal** ❑ **Family Treasures**
❑ **Furniture** ❑ **Guns** ❑ **Jewelry** ❑ **Silver** ❑ **Other**

ITEM ______________________________

Description ______________________________

Brand name and make ______________________________

Date acquired ______________________________

for (e.g., wedding gift, anniversary gift, inherited from someone, etc.) ______________________________

____

____

and current location ______________________________ (where you can find it)

Appraisal by ______________________________

on ______________ (date) is located: ______________________________

Desired beneficiary/beneficiaries, and why ______________________________

____

____

Is it a treasure? If so, explain (dollar or sentimental value): ______________

____

____

My husband still has the BB gun his dad gave him for his 6th birthday.

❑ I have included a photograph of it. ______________________________

____

❑ **Coins** ❑ **Collectibles** ❑ **China** ❑ **Crystal** ❑ **Family Treasures**
❑ **Furniture** ❑ **Guns** ❑ **Jewelry** ❑ **Silver** ❑ **Other**

ITEM ______________________________

Description ______________________________

Brand name and make ______________________________

Date acquired ______________________________

for (e.g., wedding gift, anniversary gift, inherited from someone, etc.) ______________________________

____

____

and current location ______________________________ (where you can find it)

Appraisal by ______________________________

on ____________ (date) is located: ______________________________

Desired beneficiary/beneficiaries, and why ______________________________

____

____

Is it a treasure? If so, explain (dollar or sentimental value): ______________________________

____

____

❑ I have included a photograph of it. ______________________________

____

❑ Coins ❑ Collectibles ❑ China ❑ Crystal ❑ Family Treasures
❑ Furniture ❑ Guns ❑ Jewelry ❑ Silver ❑ Other

ITEM ______________________________

Description ______________________________

Brand name and make ______________________________

Date acquired ______________________________

for (e.g., wedding gift, anniversary gift, inherited from someone, etc.) ______________________________

____

____

and current location ______________________________ (where you can find it)

Appraisal by ______________________________

on ______________ (date) is located: ______________________________

Desired beneficiary/beneficiaries, and why ______________________________

____

____

Is it a treasure? If so, explain (dollar or sentimental value): ______________________________

____

____

❑ I have included a photograph of it. ______________________________

____

❑ **Coins** ❑ **Collectibles** ❑ **China** ❑ **Crystal** ❑ **Family Treasures**
❑ **Furniture** ❑ **Guns** ❑ **Jewelry** ❑ **Silver** ❑ **Other**

ITEM ____

Description ____

Brand name and make ____

Date acquired ____

for (e.g., wedding gift, anniversary gift, inherited from someone, etc.) ____

____

____

and current location ______________________________ (where you can find it)

Appraisal by ____

on ______________ (date) is located: ______________________________

Desired beneficiary/beneficiaries, and why ____

____

____

Is it a treasure? If so, explain (dollar or sentimental value): ____

____

____

❑ I have included a photograph of it. ____

____

❑ **Coins** ❑ **Collectibles** ❑ **China** ❑ **Crystal** ❑ **Family Treasures**
❑ **Furniture** ❑ **Guns** ❑ **Jewelry** ❑ **Silver** ❑ **Other**

ITEM ____

Description ____

Brand name and make ____

Date acquired ____

for (e.g., wedding gift, anniversary gift, inherited from someone, etc.) ____________________

____

____

and current location ______________________________ (where you can find it)

Appraisal by ____

on ____________ (date) is located: ______________________________

Desired beneficiary/beneficiaries, and why ______________________________

____

____

Is it a treasure? If so, explain (dollar or sentimental value): ____________________

____

____

❑ I have included a photograph of it. ______________________________

____

❑ **Coins** ❑ **Collectibles** ❑ **China** ❑ **Crystal** ❑ **Family Treasures**

❑ **Furniture** ❑ **Guns** ❑ **Jewelry** ❑ **Silver** ❑ **Other**

ITEM ____

Description ____

Brand name and make ____

Date acquired ____

for (e.g., wedding gift, anniversary gift, inherited from someone, etc.) ______________________

____

____

and current location ______________________________ (where you can find it)

Appraisal by ____

on ______________ (date) is located: ______________________________

Desired beneficiary/beneficiaries, and why ______________________________

____

____

Is it a treasure? If so, explain (dollar or sentimental value): ______________________

____

____

❑ I have included a photograph of it. ______________________________

____

❑ **Coins** ❑ **Collectibles** ❑ **China** ❑ **Crystal** ❑ **Family Treasures**
❑ **Furniture** ❑ **Guns** ❑ **Jewelry** ❑ **Silver** ❑ **Other**

ITEM ____________________

Description ____________________

Brand name and make ____________________

Date acquired ____________________

for (e.g., wedding gift, anniversary gift, inherited from someone, etc.) ____________________

____

____

and current location ____________________ (where you can find it)

Appraisal by ____________________

on ____________ (date) is located: ____________________

Desired beneficiary/beneficiaries, and why ____________________

____

____

Is it a treasure? If so, explain (dollar or sentimental value): ____________________

____

____

❑ I have included a photograph of it. ____________________

____

❑ Coins ❑ Collectibles ❑ China ❑ Crystal ❑ Family Treasures
❑ Furniture ❑ Guns ❑ Jewelry ❑ Silver ❑ Other

ITEM ______________________________

Description ______________________________

Brand name and make ______________________________

Date acquired ______________________________

for (e.g., wedding gift, anniversary gift, inherited from someone, etc.) ______________________________

____

____

and current location ______________________________ (where you can find it)

Appraisal by ______________________________

on ______________ (date) is located: ______________________________

Desired beneficiary/beneficiaries, and why ______________________________

____

____

Is it a treasure? If so, explain (dollar or sentimental value): ______________________________

____

____

❑ I have included a photograph of it. ______________________________

____

❑ **Coins** ❑ **Collectibles** ❑ **China** ❑ **Crystal** ❑ **Family Treasures**
❑ **Furniture** ❑ **Guns** ❑ **Jewelry** ❑ **Silver** ❑ **Other**

ITEM ____

Description ____

Brand name and make ____

Date acquired ____

for (e.g., wedding gift, anniversary gift, inherited from someone, etc.) ______________________________

____

____

and current location ______________________________ (where you can find it)

Appraisal by ____

on ______________ (date) is located: ______________________________

Desired beneficiary/beneficiaries, and why ______________________________

____

____

Is it a treasure? If so, explain (dollar or sentimental value): ______________________________

____

____

❑ I have included a photograph of it. ______________________________

____

❑ **Coins** ❑ **Collectibles** ❑ **China** ❑ **Crystal** ❑ **Family Treasures**

❑ **Furniture** ❑ **Guns** ❑ **Jewelry** ❑ **Silver** ❑ **Other**

ITEM ____

Description ____

Brand name and make ____

Date acquired ____

for (e.g., wedding gift, anniversary gift, inherited from someone, etc.) ____

____

____

and current location ____ (where you can find it)

Appraisal by ____

on ______________ (date) is located: ____

Desired beneficiary/beneficiaries, and why ____

____

____

Is it a treasure? If so, explain (dollar or sentimental value): ____

____

____

❑ I have included a photograph of it. ____

____

❑ **Coins** ❑ **Collectibles** ❑ **China** ❑ **Crystal** ❑ **Family Treasures**
❑ **Furniture** ❑ **Guns** ❑ **Jewelry** ❑ **Silver** ❑ **Other**

ITEM ____________________

Description ____________________

Brand name and make ____________________

Date acquired ____________________

for (e.g., wedding gift, anniversary gift, inherited from someone, etc.) ____________________

____

____

and current location ____________________ (where you can find it)

Appraisal by ____________________

on ____________ (date) is located: ____________________

Desired beneficiary/beneficiaries, and why ____________________

____

____

Is it a treasure? If so, explain (dollar or sentimental value): ____________________

____

____

❑ I have included a photograph of it. ____________________

____

❑ **Coins** ❑ **Collectibles** ❑ **China** ❑ **Crystal** ❑ **Family Treasures**
❑ **Furniture** ❑ **Guns** ❑ **Jewelry** ❑ **Silver** ❑ **Other**

ITEM ____

Description ____

Brand name and make ____

Date acquired ____

for (e.g., wedding gift, anniversary gift, inherited from someone, etc.) ____

____

____

and current location ____ (where you can find it)

Appraisal by ____

on ______________ (date) is located: ____

Desired beneficiary/beneficiaries, and why ____

____

____

Is it a treasure? If so, explain (dollar or sentimental value): ____

____

____

❑ I have included a photograph of it. ____

____

❑ **Coins** ❑ **Collectibles** ❑ **China** ❑ **Crystal** ❑ **Family Treasures**
❑ **Furniture** ❑ **Guns** ❑ **Jewelry** ❑ **Silver** ❑ **Other**

ITEM ____________________

Description ____________________

Brand name and make ____________________

Date acquired ____________________

for (e.g., wedding gift, anniversary gift, inherited from someone, etc.) ____________________

____

____

and current location ____________________ (where you can find it)

Appraisal by ____________________

on ____________ (date) is located: ____________________

Desired beneficiary/beneficiaries, and why ____________________

____

____

Is it a treasure? If so, explain (dollar or sentimental value): ____________________

____

____

❑ I have included a photograph of it. ____________________

____

❑ Coins ❑ Collectibles ❑ China ❑ Crystal ❑ Family Treasures

❑ Furniture ❑ Guns ❑ Jewelry ❑ Silver ❑ Other

ITEM ______________________________

Description ______________________________

Brand name and make ______________________________

Date acquired ______________________________

for (e.g., wedding gift, anniversary gift, inherited from someone, etc.) ______________

____

____

and current location ______________ (where you can find it)

Appraisal by ______________________________

on ____________(date) is located: ______________

Every piece of jewelry has a story. One of my grandmothers wrote long notes and safety pinned them to each item. I treasure these notes in her handwriting.

Desired beneficiary/beneficiaries, and why ______________________________

____

____

Is it a treasure? If so, explain (dollar or sentimental value): ______________

____

____

❑ I have included a photograph of it. ______________________________

____

❑ **Coins** ❑ **Collectibles** ❑ **China** ❑ **Crystal** ❑ **Family Treasures**
❑ **Furniture** ❑ **Guns** ❑ **Jewelry** ❑ **Silver** ❑ **Other**

ITEM ____

Description ____

Brand name and make ____

Date acquired ____

for (e.g., wedding gift, anniversary gift, inherited from someone, etc.) ____________________

____

____

and current location ______________________________ (where you can find it)

Appraisal by ____

on ______________ (date) is located: ______________________________

Desired beneficiary/beneficiaries, and why ______________________________

____

____

Is it a treasure? If so, explain (dollar or sentimental value): ____________________

____

____

❑ I have included a photograph of it. ______________________________

____

❑ **Coins** ❑ **Collectibles** ❑ **China** ❑ **Crystal** ❑ **Family Treasures**
❑ **Furniture** ❑ **Guns** ❑ **Jewelry** ❑ **Silver** ❑ **Other**

ITEM ____

Description ____

Brand name and make ____

Date acquired ____

for (e.g., wedding gift, anniversary gift, inherited from someone, etc.) ______________________

____

____

and current location ______________________________ (where you can find it)

Appraisal by ____

on ______________ (date) is located: ______________________________

Desired beneficiary/beneficiaries, and why ______________________________

____

____

Is it a treasure? If so, explain (dollar or sentimental value): ______________________

____

____

❑ I have included a photograph of it. ______________________________

____

❑ **Coins** ❑ **Collectibles** ❑ **China** ❑ **Crystal** ❑ **Family Treasures**
❑ **Furniture** ❑ **Guns** ❑ **Jewelry** ❑ **Silver** ❑ **Other**

ITEM ______________________________

Description ______________________________

Brand name and make ______________________________

Date acquired ______________________________

for (e.g., wedding gift, anniversary gift, inherited from someone, etc.) ______________________________

____

____

and current location ______________________________ (where you can find it)

Appraisal by ______________________________

on ______________ (date) is located: ______________________________

Desired beneficiary/beneficiaries, and why ______________________________

____

____

Is it a treasure? If so, explain (dollar or sentimental value): ______________________________

____

____

❑ I have included a photograph of it. ______________________________

____

There was a time when my mom hid jewelry in a cereal box! If you didn't know, you just might throw out that cereal!

❑ **Coins** ❑ **Collectibles** ❑ **China** ❑ **Crystal** ❑ **Family Treasures**
❑ **Furniture** ❑ **Guns** ❑ **Jewelry** ❑ **Silver** ❑ **Other**

ITEM ____

Description ____

Brand name and make ____

Date acquired ____

for (e.g., wedding gift, anniversary gift, inherited from someone, etc.) ____

____

____

and current location ______________________________ (where you can find it)

Appraisal by ____

on ______________ (date) is located: ______________________________

Desired beneficiary/beneficiaries, and why ______________________________

____

____

Is it a treasure? If so, explain (dollar or sentimental value): ______________________________

____

____

❑ I have included a photograph of it. ______________________________

____

❑ **Coins** ❑ **Collectibles** ❑ **China** ❑ **Crystal** ❑ **Family Treasures**
❑ **Furniture** ❑ **Guns** ❑ **Jewelry** ❑ **Silver** ❑ **Other**

ITEM ____

Description ____

Brand name and make ____

Date acquired ____

for (e.g., wedding gift, anniversary gift, inherited from someone, etc.) ____________________

____

____

and current location ______________________________ (where you can find it)

Appraisal by ____

on ______________ (date) is located: ______________________________

Desired beneficiary/beneficiaries, and why ____________________

____

____

Is it a treasure? If so, explain (dollar or sentimental value): ____________________

____

____

❑ I have included a photograph of it. ______________________________

____

❑ **Coins** ❑ **Collectibles** ❑ **China** ❑ **Crystal** ❑ **Family Treasures**

❑ **Furniture** ❑ **Guns** ❑ **Jewelry** ❑ **Silver** ❑ **Other**

ITEM ____

Description ____

Brand name and make ____

Date acquired ____

for (e.g., wedding gift, anniversary gift, inherited from someone, etc.) ______________________

____

____

and current location ______________________________ (where you can find it)

Appraisal by ____

on ______________ (date) is located: ______________________________

Desired beneficiary/beneficiaries, and why ______________________________

____

____

Is it a treasure? If so, explain (dollar or sentimental value): ______________________

____

____

❑ I have included a photograph of it. ______________________________

____

❑ **Coins** ❑ **Collectibles** ❑ **China** ❑ **Crystal** ❑ **Family Treasures**
❑ **Furniture** ❑ **Guns** ❑ **Jewelry** ❑ **Silver** ❑ **Other**

ITEM ______________________________

Description ______________________________

Brand name and make ______________________________

Date acquired ______________________________

for (e.g., wedding gift, anniversary gift, inherited from someone, etc.) ______________________________

____

____

and current location ______________________________ (where you can find it)

Appraisal by ______________________________

on ____________ (date) is located: ______________________________

Desired beneficiary/beneficiaries, and why ______________________________

____

____

Is it a treasure? If so, explain (dollar or sentimental value): ______________________________

____

____

❑ I have included a photograph of it. ______________________________

____

❑ **Coins** ❑ **Collectibles** ❑ **China** ❑ **Crystal** ❑ **Family Treasures**
❑ **Furniture** ❑ **Guns** ❑ **Jewelry** ❑ **Silver** ❑ **Other**

ITEM ____

Description ____

Brand name and make ____

Date acquired ____

for (e.g., wedding gift, anniversary gift, inherited from someone, etc.) ______________________

____

____

and current location ______________________________ (where you can find it)

Appraisal by ____

on ______________ (date) is located: ______________________________

Desired beneficiary/beneficiaries, and why ______________________________

____

____

Is it a treasure? If so, explain (dollar or sentimental value): ______________________

____

____

❑ I have included a photograph of it. ______________________________

____

❑ **Coins** ❑ **Collectibles** ❑ **China** ❑ **Crystal** ❑ **Family Treasures**
❑ **Furniture** ❑ **Guns** ❑ **Jewelry** ❑ **Silver** ❑ **Other**

ITEM ______________________________

Description ______________________________

Brand name and make ______________________________

Date acquired ______________________________

for (e.g., wedding gift, anniversary gift, inherited from someone, etc.) ______________________________

____

____

and current location ______________________________ (where you can find it)

Appraisal by ______________________________

on ____________ (date) is located: ______________________________

Desired beneficiary/beneficiaries, and why ______________________________

____

____

Is it a treasure? If so, explain (dollar or sentimental value): ______________________________

____

____

❑ I have included a photograph of it. ______________________________

____

❑ **Coins** ❑ **Collectibles** ❑ **China** ❑ **Crystal** ❑ **Family Treasures**

❑ **Furniture** ❑ **Guns** ❑ **Jewelry** ❑ **Silver** ❑ **Other**

ITEM ____

Description ____

Brand name and make ____

Date acquired ____

for (e.g., wedding gift, anniversary gift, inherited from someone, etc.) ______________________

____

____

and current location ______________________________ (where you can find it)

Appraisal by ____

on ______________ (date) is located: ______________________________

Desired beneficiary/beneficiaries, and why ______________________________

____

____

Is it a treasure? If so, explain (dollar or sentimental value): ______________________

____

____

❑ I have included a photograph of it. ______________________________

____

❑ **Coins** ❑ **Collectibles** ❑ **China** ❑ **Crystal** ❑ **Family Treasures**
❑ **Furniture** ❑ **Guns** ❑ **Jewelry** ❑ **Silver** ❑ **Other**

ITEM ____

Description ____

Brand name and make ____

Date acquired ____

for (e.g., wedding gift, anniversary gift, inherited from someone, etc.) ______________________

____

____

and current location ______________________________ (where you can find it)

Appraisal by ____

on ______________ (date) is located: ______________________________

Desired beneficiary/beneficiaries, and why ______________________________

____

____

Is it a treasure? If so, explain (dollar or sentimental value): ______________________

____

____

❑ I have included a photograph of it. ______________________________

____

❑ **Coins** ❑ **Collectibles** ❑ **China** ❑ **Crystal** ❑ **Family Treasures**
❑ **Furniture** ❑ **Guns** ❑ **Jewelry** ❑ **Silver** ❑ **Other**

ITEM ____

Description ____

Brand name and make ____

Date acquired ____

for (e.g., wedding gift, anniversary gift, inherited from someone, etc.) ____________________

____

____

and current location ______________________________ (where you can find it)

Appraisal by ____

on ______________ (date) is located: ______________________________

Desired beneficiary/beneficiaries, and why ______________________________

____

____

Is it a treasure? If so, explain (dollar or sentimental value): ____________________

____

____

❑ I have included a photograph of it. ______________________________

____

❑ **Coins** ❑ **Collectibles** ❑ **China** ❑ **Crystal** ❑ **Family Treasures**
❑ **Furniture** ❑ **Guns** ❑ **Jewelry** ❑ **Silver** ❑ **Other**

ITEM ____

Description ____

Brand name and make ____

Date acquired ____

for (e.g., wedding gift, anniversary gift, inherited from someone, etc.) ______________________________

____

____

and current location ______________________________ (where you can find it)

Appraisal by ____

on ____________ (date) is located: ______________________________

Desired beneficiary/beneficiaries, and why ______________________________

____

____

Is it a treasure? If so, explain (dollar or sentimental value): ______________________________

____

____

❑ I have included a photograph of it. ______________________________

____

Land

I own land in the following locations, and you can find the deeds and title insurance for each parcel as I've listed it.

____ (address)

I own this property ❑ individually ❑ jointly ____________________

with ____

or ❑ as community property with __________________________

Brief description: ___________________________________

Acquisition date ___________________ and cost _____________

The deed can be found in ________________________________

Title insurance can be found in ____________________________

The mortgage is through __________________________ (institution)

at ______________________________(address)____________________ (phone number)

The mortgage paperwork can be found ____

Desired beneficiary/beneficiaries: and why ____

____

Is it a treasure? If so, explain (dollar value or sentimental): ______________________________

____

❑ I have included a photograph of it. ______________________________________

As you fill out this section, include any real estate you own individually, jointly (with someone else), and any time-shares you own or have an interest in.

Land

______________________________ (address)

____

I own this property ❑ individually ❑ jointly ______________________________

with ______________________________

or ❑ as community property with ______________________________

Brief description: ______________________________

Acquisition date ______________ and cost ______________

The deed can be found in ______________________________

Title insurance can be found in ______________________________

The mortgage is through ______________ (institution) ______________

at ______________ (address) ______________ (phone number)

The mortgage paperwork can be found ______________________________

Desired beneficiary/beneficiaries: and why ______________________________

____

Is it a treasure? If so, explain (dollar value or sentimental): ______________________________

____

____

❑ I have included a photograph of it. ______________________________

Land

______________________________ (address)

____

I own this property ❑ individually ❑ jointly ______________________________

with ______________________________

or ❑ as community property with ______________________________

Brief description: ______________________________

Acquisition date ______________ and cost ______________

The deed can be found in ______________________________

Title insurance can be found in ______________________________

The mortgage is through ______________ (institution)

at ______________ (address) ______________ (phone number)

The mortgage paperwork can be found ______________________________

Desired beneficiary/beneficiaries: and why ______________________________

____

Is it a treasure? If so, explain (dollar value or sentimental): ______________

____

____

❑ I have included a photograph of it. ______________________________

We own a house at Lake Lotawana. My grandmother saved her knitting money to buy the first family home (TINY) there. That single act created a lifestyle change for all her children and grandchildren. Most own homes on lakes somewhere!

Land

____ (address)

____

I own this property ❑ individually ❑ jointly ____________________

with ____

or ❑ as community property with __________________________

Brief description: __________________________________

Acquisition date ________________ and cost ____________________

The deed can be found in ______________________________

Title insurance can be found in ____________________________

The mortgage is through ______________________________ (institution)

at ________________________ (address) ________________ (phone number)

The mortgage paperwork can be found ____________________

Desired beneficiary/beneficiaries: and why __________________

____

Is it a treasure? If so, explain (dollar value or sentimental): __________

____

____

❑ I have included a photograph of it. ____________________

Be sure to tell stories about fun trips to your places, or how your property was "discovered." This rich history is so meaningful!

Land

____ (address)

____

I own this property ❑ individually ❑ jointly ____________________

with ____________________________________

or ❑ as community property with ________________________

Brief description: ______________________________

Acquisition date ______________ and cost __________________

The deed can be found in __________________________

Title insurance can be found in ________________________

The mortgage is through ________________________ (institution)

at ____________________ (address) ______________(phone number)

The mortgage paperwork can be found ______________________

Desired beneficiary/beneficiaries: and why ____________________

____

Is it a treasure? If so, explain (dollar value or sentimental): ______________

____

____

❑ I have included a photograph of it. ______________________

Land

____ (address)

____

I own this property ❑ individually ❑ jointly _______________

with ____

or ❑ as community property with _______________________

Brief description: _______________________________________

Acquisition date _______________ and cost _______________

The deed can be found in _________________________________

Title insurance can be found in ___________________________

The mortgage is through ______________________ (institution)

at ______________________ (address) ______________ (phone number)

The mortgage paperwork can be found ______________________

Desired beneficiary/beneficiaries: and why ________________

____

Is it a treasure? If so, explain (dollar value or sentimental): ____________

____

____

❑ I have included a photograph of it. ______________________

Motors and Wheels

Make, Model and VIN ___________________________

Description ___________________________

Located ___________________________

You can find the keys ___________________________

I keep the title ___________________________

I owe money to ___________________________(lender)

Located at ___________________(address) ______________(phone number)

❑ I have included a photograph of it. ___________________________

Cars, trucks, RVs, and motorized toys (boats, motorcycles, airplanes, or other toys – include sailboats and canoes or kayaks even though they don't have motors) belong right here!

Make, Model and VIN ___________________________

Description ___________________________

Located ___________________________

You can find the keys ___________________________

I keep the title ___________________________

I owe money to ___________________________(lender)

Located at ___________________(address) ______________(phone number)

❑ I have included a photograph of it. ___________________________

Motors and Wheels

Make, Model and VIN ____________________

Description ____________________

Located ____________________

You can find the keys ____________________

I keep the title ____________________

I owe money to ____________________ (lender)

Located at ____________________ (address) ____________________ (phone number)

❑ I have included a photograph of it. ____________________

____

____

Make, Model and VIN ____________________

Description ____________________

Located ____________________

You can find the keys ____________________

I keep the title ____________________

I owe money to ____________________ (lender)

Located at ____________________ (address) ____________________ (phone number)

❑ I have included a photograph of it. ____________________

Motors and Wheels

Make, Model and VIN ______________________________

Description ______________________________

Located ______________________________

You can find the keys ______________________________

I keep the title ______________________________

I owe money to ______________________________ (lender)

Located at ______________________________ (address) ______________ (phone number)

❑ I have included a photograph of it. ______________________________

Make, Model and VIN ______________________________

Description ______________________________

Located ______________________________

You can find the keys ______________________________

I keep the title ______________________________

I owe money to ______________________________ (lender)

Located at ______________________________ (address) ______________ (phone number)

❑ I have included a photograph of it. ______________________________

Motors and Wheels

Make, Model and VIN ______________________________

Description ______________________________

Located ______________________________

You can find the keys ______________________________

I keep the title ______________________________

I owe money to ______________________________ (lender)

Located at ____________________ (address) ____________ (phone number)

❑ I have included a photograph of it. ______________________________

Make, Model and VIN ______________________________

Description ______________________________

Located ______________________________

You can find the keys ______________________________

I keep the title ______________________________

I owe money to ______________________________ (lender)

Located at ____________________ (address) ____________ (phone number)

❑ I have included a photograph of it. ______________________________

The Rest of My Stuff

ITEM ______________________________

Description ______________________________

____

____

Date completed ______________________________

____

Current location ______________________________ (where you can find it)

____

Appraisal by ______________________________ on ______________ (date)

Located: ______________________________

Desired beneficiary/beneficiaries, and why ______________________________

____

____

Is it a treasure? If so, explain (dollar or sentimental value): ______________

____

____

____

❑ I have included a photograph of it. ______________________________

This is where rugs and precious metals that aren't jewelry should be listed.

The Rest of My Stuff

I'm thinking special holiday décor. – You know. Some of it is really special, and I only put it out for a few days each year.

ITEM ____________________

Description ____________________

____

____

Date completed ____________________

____

Current location ____________________ (where you can find it)

____

Appraisal by ____________________ on ____________________ (date)

Located: ____________________

Desired beneficiary/beneficiaries, and why ____________________

____

____

Is it a treasure? If so, explain (dollar or sentimental value): ____________________

____

____

____

❑ I have included a photograph of it. ____________________

The Rest of My Stuff

My cowboy boots are precious to me and they are my trademark. Only one person wants them. Luckily we wear the same size!

ITEM ______________________________

Description ______________________________

____

____

Date completed ______________________________

____

Current location ______________________ (where you can find it)

____

Appraisal by ______________ on ______________ (date)

Located: ______________________________

Desired beneficiary/beneficiaries, and why ______________________________

____

____

Is it a treasure? If so, explain (dollar or sentimental value): ______________________________

____

____

____

❑ I have included a photograph of it. ______________________________

The Rest of My Stuff

ITEM ______________________________

Description ______________________________

____

____

Date completed ______________________________

____

Current location ______________________________ (where you can find it)

____

Appraisal by ______________________ on ______________ (date)

Located: ______________________________

Desired beneficiary/beneficiaries, and why ______________________________

____

____

Is it a treasure? If so, explain (dollar or sentimental value): ______________________________

____

____

____

❑ I have included a photograph of it. ______________________________

The Rest of My Stuff

ITEM ______________________________

Description ______________________________

____

____

Date completed ______________________________

____

Current location ______________________________ (where you can find it)

____

Appraisal by ______________________________ on ______________ (date)

Located: ______________________________

Desired beneficiary/beneficiaries, and why ______________________________

____

____

Is it a treasure? If so, explain (dollar or sentimental value): ______________________________

____

____

____

❑ I have included a photograph of it. ______________________________

The Rest of My Stuff

ITEM ______

Description ______

______

______

Date completed ______

______

Current location ______ (where you can find it)

______

Appraisal by ______ on ______ (date)

Located: ______

Desired beneficiary/beneficiaries, and why ______

______

______

Is it a treasure? If so, explain (dollar or sentimental value): ______

______

______

______

❑ I have included a photograph of it. ______

The Rest of My Stuff

ITEM ______________________________

Description ______________________________

____

____

Date completed ______________________________

____

Current location ______________________________ (where you can find it)

____

Appraisal by ______________________________ on ______________ (date)

Located: ______________________________

Desired beneficiary/beneficiaries, and why ______________________________

____

____

Is it a treasure? If so, explain (dollar or sentimental value): ______________________________

____

____

____

❑ I have included a photograph of it. ______________________________

The Rest of My Stuff

ITEM ____________________

Description ____________________

____

____

Date completed ____________________

____

Current location ____________________ (where you can find it)

____

Appraisal by ____________________ on ____________ (date)

Located: ____________________

Desired beneficiary/beneficiaries, and why ____________________

____

____

Is it a treasure? If so, explain (dollar or sentimental value): ____________________

____

____

____

❑ I have included a photograph of it. ____________________

There are worse things in life than death. Have you ever spent an evening with an insurance salesman?

Woody Allen

CHAPTER

9

Insurance

You can list all your insurance coverage here.

For My Care

HEALTH

Policy Description ______________________________

Policy Number ______________________________

Insurance Company ______________________________

Insurance Agent ______________________________

Phone Number ______________________________

Email Address ______________________________

Street Address ______________________________

Location of Policy ______________________________

HEALTH

Policy Description ______________________________

Policy Number ______________________________

Insurance Company ______________________________

Insurance Agent ______________________________

Phone Number ______________________________

Email Address ______________________________

Street Address ______________________________

Location of Policy ______________________________

For My Care

MEDICARE/MEDICAID

Description/Type ______________________________

Policy Number ______________________________

Insurance Company______________________________

Contact ______________________________

Phone Number______________________________

Email Address ______________________________

Street Address______________________________

Location of Policy______________________________

MEDICARE/MEDICAID

Description/Type ______________________________

Policy Number ______________________________

Insurance Company ______________________________

Contact ______________________________

Phone Number ______________________________

Email Address ______________________________

Street Address ______________________________

Location of Policy ______________________________

For My Care

DISABILITY

Policy Description ______

Policy Number ______

Insurance Company ______

Insurance Agent ______

Phone Number ______

Email Address ______

Street Address ______

Location of Policy ______

DISABILITY

Policy Description ______

Policy Number ______

Insurance Company ______

Insurance Agent ______

Phone Number ______

Email Address ______

Street Address ______

Location of Policy ______

For My Care

LONG-TERM CARE

Policy Description ______________________________

Policy Number ______________________________

Insurance Company ______________________________

Insurance Agent ______________________________

Phone Number ______________________________

Email Address ______________________________

Street Address ______________________________

Location of Policy ______________________________

LONG-TERM CARE

Policy Description ______________________________

Policy Number ______________________________

Insurance Company ______________________________

Insurance Agent ______________________________

Phone Number ______________________________

Email Address ______________________________

Street Address ______________________________

Location of Policy ______________________________

For My Life

LIFE INSURANCE

Policy Description ____________________

Policy Number ____________________

Insurance Company ____________________

Insurance Agent ____________________ Phone Number ____________________

Email Address ____________________ Street Address ____________________

Location of Policy ____________________

Beneficiary(ies) ____________________

Type of Policy (whole life/variable life, etc.) ____________________ Dollar Value ____________________

LIFE INSURANCE

Policy Description ____________________

Policy Number ____________________

Insurance Company ____________________

Insurance Agent ____________________ Phone Number ____________________

Email Address ____________________ Street Address ____________________

Location of Policy ____________________

Beneficiary(ies) ____________________

Type of Policy (whole life/variable life, etc.) ____________________ Dollar Value ____________________

For My Life

LIFE INSURANCE

Policy Description ____________________

Policy Number ____________________

Insurance Company ____________________

Insurance Agent ____________________ Phone Number ____________________

Email Address ____________________ Street Address ____________________

Location of Policy ____________________

Beneficiary(ies) ____________________

Type of Policy (whole life/variable life, etc.) ____________________ Dollar Value ____________________

LIFE INSURANCE

Policy Description ____________________

Policy Number ____________________

Insurance Company ____________________

Insurance Agent ____________________ Phone Number ____________________

Email Address ____________________ Street Address ____________________

Location of Policy ____________________

Beneficiary(ies) ____________________

Type of Policy (whole life/variable life, etc.) ____________________ Dollar Value ____________________

For My Property

HOMEOWNERS

Policy Description (for which location/house) ____________________

Policy Number ____________________

Insurance Company ____________________ Insurance Agent ____________________

Phone Number ____________________ Email Address ____________________

Street Address ____________________

Location of Policy ____________________

Annual Cost ____________________ Policy Limits ____________________

____

HOMEOWNERS

Policy Description (for which location/house) ____________________

Policy Number ____________________

Insurance Company ____________________ Insurance Agent ____________________

Phone Number ____________________ Email Address ____________________

Street Address ____________________

Location of Policy ____________________

Annual Cost ____________________ Policy Limits ____________________

____

For My Property

HOMEOWNERS

Policy Description (for which location/house) ____________________

Policy Number ____________________

Insurance Company ____________________ Insurance Agent ____________________

Phone Number ____________________ Email Address ____________________

Street Address ____________________

Location of Policy ____________________

Annual Cost ____________________ Policy Limits ____________________

____

HOMEOWNERS

Policy Description (for which location/house) ____________________

Policy Number ____________________

Insurance Company ____________________ Insurance Agent ____________________

Phone Number ____________________ Email Address ____________________

Street Address ____________________

Location of Policy ____________________

Annual Cost ____________________ Policy Limits ____________________

____

For My Property

AUTO

Policy Description (for which location/house) ______________________________

Policy Number ______________________________

Insurance Company ______________ Insurance Agent ______________

Phone Number ______________ Email Address ______________

Street Address ______________________________

Location of Policy ______________________________

Annual Cost ______________ Policy Limits ______________

____

AUTO

Policy Description (for which location/house) ______________________________

Policy Number ______________________________

Insurance Company ______________ Insurance Agent ______________

Phone Number ______________ Email Address ______________

Street Address ______________________________

Location of Policy ______________________________

Annual Cost ______________ Policy Limits ______________

____

For My Property

AUTO

Policy Description (for which location/house) ______________________

Policy Number ______________________

Insurance Company ______________ Insurance Agent ______________

Phone Number ______________ Email Address ______________

Street Address ______________________

Location of Policy ______________________

Annual Cost ______________ Policy Limits ______________

____

AUTO

Policy Description (for which location/house) ______________________

Policy Number ______________________

Insurance Company ______________ Insurance Agent ______________

Phone Number ______________ Email Address ______________

Street Address ______________________

Location of Policy ______________________

Annual Cost ______________ Policy Limits ______________

____

Umbrella Insurance

(No, this isn't insurance on your favorite umbrella! It is the extra piece they put in place above and beyond your other insurance to give you higher limits! It protects you like an umbrella.)

Policy Description (for which location/house) ____________________

Policy Number ____________________

Insurance Company ____________________ Insurance Agent ____________________

Phone Number ____________________ Email Address ____________________

Street Address ____________________

Location of Policy ____________________

Annual Cost ____________________ Policy Limits ____________________

____

Policy Description (for which location/house) ____________________

Policy Number ____________________

Insurance Company ____________________ Insurance Agent ____________________

Phone Number ____________________ Email Address ____________________

Street Address ____________________

Location of Policy ____________________

Annual Cost ____________________ Policy Limits ____________________

Special Lines Insurance

This is out-of-the-ordinary insurance. Examples include wedding insurance (think weather), travel insurance for a trip, and overseas recovery (when they transport you back to the US or to a "friendly" developed country if you become ill overseas.)

Policy Description (for which location/house) ______________________________

Policy Number ______________________________

Insurance Company ____________________ Insurance Agent ____________________

Phone Number ____________________ Email Address ____________________

Street Address ______________________________

Location of Policy ______________________________

Annual Cost ____________________ Policy Limits ____________________

____

Policy Description (for which location/house) ______________________________

Policy Number ______________________________

Insurance Company ____________________ Insurance Agent ____________________

Phone Number ____________________ Email Address ____________________

Street Address ______________________________

Location of Policy ______________________________

Annual Cost ____________________ Policy Limits ____________________

"According to most studies, peoples' number one fear is public speaking. Number two is death. This means to the average person, if you go to a funeral, you're better off in the casket than doing the eulogy."

Jerry Seinfeld

CHAPTER

10

My Little Black Book

List key contacts your people will need to find.

Business Contacts

ACCOUNTANT

Name ______________________________

Address ______________________________

Phone Number ______________________________

LAWYER

Name ______________________________

Address ______________________________

Phone Number ______________________________

FINANCIAL ADVISOR

Name ______________________________

Address ______________________________

Phone Number ______________________________

____

Additional business contacts can be found in the ______________________________

(computer, blackberry, rolodex) located on my ______________________________

____

____

____

Personal Contacts

Include your BFF, housekeeper, neighbor, building manager, tenant, service providers (lawn care, etc.) book club, church group.

Name ____

Address ______________________________________

Phone Number __________________________________

____

Name ____

Address ______________________________________

Phone Number __________________________________

____

Name ____

Address ______________________________________

Phone Number __________________________________

____

Name ____

Address ______________________________________

Phone Number __________________________________

____

Personal Contacts

Name ______________________________

Address ______________________________

Phone Number ______________________________

____

Name ______________________________

Address ______________________________

Phone Number ______________________________

____

Name ______________________________

Address ______________________________

Phone Number ______________________________

____

Name ______________________________

Address ______________________________

Phone Number ______________________________

____

____

____

Personal Contacts

Name ______________________________

Address ______________________________

Phone Number ______________________________

____

Name ______________________________

Address ______________________________

Phone Number ______________________________

____

Name ______________________________

Address ______________________________

Phone Number ______________________________

____

Name ______________________________

Address ______________________________

Phone Number ______________________________

____

____

____

Personal Contacts

Name ____________________

Address ____________________

Phone Number ____________________

____

Name ____________________

Address ____________________

Phone Number ____________________

____

Name ____________________

Address ____________________

Phone Number ____________________

____

Name ____________________

Address ____________________

Phone Number ____________________

____

____

____

Personal Contacts

Name ______________________________

Address ______________________________

Phone Number ______________________________

____

Name ______________________________

Address ______________________________

Phone Number ______________________________

____

Name ______________________________

Address ______________________________

Phone Number ______________________________

____

Name ______________________________

Address ______________________________

Phone Number ______________________________

____

____

____

*“Every man dies,
not every man
really lives.”*

William Wallace

CHAPTER

11

Spy Codes and Secret Passwords

Keep your passwords safe, but find a way to share them with loved ones after you die.

Five Tips about Codes:

1. Do not make them too complicated.
2. Do not make them too easy.
3. Use letters and numbers you already have memorized.
4. Change the factory provided code immediately.
5. Keep a password list somewhere hidden but handy.

My Passwords

Be careful about writing your passwords here. Be sure to keep this book safe if you do so.

COMPUTER PASSWORDS

The password for the computer located in the ______________________

is ______________________

The password for the computer located in the ______________________

is ______________________

The password for the computer located in the ______________________

is ______________________

For accounts you access with your computer, be sure someone knows your passwords! Consider AOL, Yahoo, financial accounts (bank accounts or auto-pay accounts, Facebook, etc.) Be careful about where you store this information. Unless you lock-up this book, this may not be the best place for this information.

Type of Account and email address	Account Name	Password

Key-Pad Codes

Be careful about writing your passwords here. Be sure to keep this book safe if you do so.

The code to the garage door key-pad is: ______________________________

____

The burglar alarm code for the ______________________________ (location)

is ______________________________

The monitoring company contact name and phone number are ______________________________

____

____

The burglar alarm code for the ______________________________ (location)

is ______________________________

The monitoring company contact name and phone number are ______________________________

____

____

____

Cell phone codes ______________________________

____

____

____

____

Other Top Secret Information

Be careful about writing your passwords here. Be sure to keep this book safe if you do so.

Other locations with key-pads and their codes are:

Location	Code	Contact Person/Phone

PART THREE

My Final Wishes

"You should always go to other peoples' funerals; otherwise they won't come to yours."

Yogi Berra

CHAPTER

12

My Fabulous Funeral

Plan this now, at least in part. You can reduce the stress on your family.

This chapter is specifically designed to tell your funeral planners exactly what you want. It is best if you plan as much as YOU can. At the very least, write down your preferences regarding burial or cremation.

This chapter makes it easy for you to help plan the services, choose speakers, readings, and even your clothing, food and notices. You can do this with the same attention to detail you did for your wedding, baby births, and milestone birthdays! You can even write your own obituary and choose the photo you want in the paper! We have included resources to help you make decisions.
It is easy and will help your friends and family immensely.

Talk to your loved ones about this chapter if you are comfortable with the subject. Saying goodbye is really difficult. Filling out these pages can make it easier on your loved ones, and on you!

My Body's Final Act

Before you plan the funeral, it is important to consider your body's final act. There are two types of donations (for transplant, and to science). They are both explained below, as is an autopsy. (see page 265).

DONATIONS FOR TRANSPLANT

Quite often after death, organs can be donated to improve the life of another human being. This requires fast action, so it helps to communicate your desires ahead of time! Skin can save a severely burned victim by serving as a temporary protective covering until their own skin grows back. A kidney, heart, lungs or pancreas can mean the difference between life and death. Corneas will let another see again. Medicine continues to evolve, making other life-altering gifts possible.

Many people take comfort knowing that we may offer life to someone else even when our own lives have ended.

You can also go to www.organdonor.gov and follow the simple process if you would like to be an organ donor. There are many ways to help others. See www.lcnw.org/donation/organs-tissues-for-transplant/.

One person can save up to eight lives through organ donation – and they can improve the lives of over a hundred people through tissue donation. Recipients might need a transplanted organ for any number of reasons, from disease to congenital defects to simple wear-and-tear.

My Wishes Regarding Donation for Transplant

☐ I want to donate my organs for transplant, and have filled out forms that can be found in

____

____

____

☐ I want to donate my organs for transplant, but have not taken any steps in the process.

☐ I do not want to donate my organs for transplant.

Be sure the proper paperwork has been filled out and is readily accessible AND that you have told your loved ones your intentions… or the donor "opportunity" may be missed!

If you don't take time to fill out an organ donor form, at least look at the back of your drivers license and check [] the right box if you want to be a donor! Thousands of people are waiting…hoping for help!

Donations to Science for Medical Research

BODY DONATION TO SCIENCE

This is different from donating your organs to be transplanted. Donating to science means your body will be available for scientific research. If you are interested in doing this, contact your local (or your favorite) university or research center now. They will have a form for you to fill out (now) so that proper steps can be taken. Delivery of the body usually must occur within 24 hours of death, and your body must not have been embalmed.

The funeral home can usually transfer your body to the science department. Each research center/university has a different process. Be sure to check their website and fill out the appropriate information. Then place the completed form in this notebook. Donations to science can also sometimes be accomplished after your death if you have not prepared the paperwork – if all the people involved agree "soon enough." The process will be much less confusing, however, if you complete the forms ahead of time and share the information with your loved ones.

For more information, search "donate body to science process" on your computer or visit sites like these: www.MedCure.org, www.sciencecare.com (if you live in AZ, CA, CO, FL or TX).

My mom has decided to donate her body to Mayo Clinic. I was relieved to (1) know her wishes, and (2) understand how the process works so when the time comes I can more easily implement her plan.

Donations to Science for Medical Research

BRAIN DONATION TO SCIENCE

Medical schools and research institutes need brain tissue for studies on neurological disorders like dementia, autism, and narcolepsy, so they make the process of brain donation free and easy to coordinate. Because it does not typically interfere with standard funeral arrangements, brain donation provides an alternative to full body donation. Total body donors cannot have a traditional viewing (because the body can not be embalmed) or burial. Brain donors can still have an open-casket viewing and a traditional interment.

For information, search "donate brain" on your computer or visit sites like this one: www.brainbank.mclean.org

I wonder if my brain will be more helpful DONATED than it is to me today? Hmmm…

MY WISHES REGARDING DONATION TO SCIENCE

❑ I want to donate my body to science, and have filled out forms that can be found in

____

I have arranged for it to be sent to ______________________ (medical center or institute).

❑ I want to donate my brain only to science, and have filled out forms that can be found in

____

I have arranged for it to be sent to ______________________ (medical center or institute).

____

❑ I want to donate ❑ my body to science OR ❑ my brain to science, but have not taken any steps in the process.

❑ I do not want to donate my body or brain to science.

Autopsy

In some cases, an autopsy will be performed at the direction of the authorities. Autopsies are commonly ordered if there was foul play, if there is a public health concern, or if a physician is uncomfortable signing a death certificate with a specific cause.

If an autopsy is not ordered, the next-of-kin can request one. If the decedent was in a hospital, the hospital will often perform the autopsy free of charge. If a "free" autopsy is not available (or the family would prefer an autopsy performed by a different facility), the next-of-kin can pay for a private autopsy. An autopsy may also be helpful for insurance purposes. If there may have been medical malpractice leading to the death, an autopsy could help prove the case. When in doubt, call an attorney for guidance.

The National Association of Medical Examiners provides a list of autopsy providers without endorsing any group or individual. Go to www.thename.org and select "private autopsies."

MY WISHES REGARDING AN AUTOPSY

❑ I definitely want an autopsy if one is not completed as a matter of routine.

❑ I don't have an opinion about an autopsy if one is not completed as a matter of routine.

Burial and Cremation Options

Selecting a final "resting place" can be an emotionally charged decision. This section is merely meant to provide you with an overview of some of the available options. While burial and cremation seem "simple," there are now many interesting options within each category! (And you can even combine a casket and viewing with cremation.) The trend toward eco-burials is also relatively new (or shall we say revived since the have been around for thousands of years before fancy caskets and vaults), and growing in popularity.

Burial and Cremation Options

BURIAL IN A CASKET (to be taken to a cemetery, or placed in a crypt)

- The casket can range from simple (pine box) to elaborate, specially designed caskets
- This can be accomplished with or without a headstone or marker
- Some people place the casket in an airtight “vault” for burial

ECO OR GREEN BURIAL (body wrapped in a covering without a casket) either with or without a marker. Green burials are designed to ensure that the burial site remains as natural as possible. Embalming fluid and concrete vaults are not utilized. While this may seem “new,” it really isn’t!

www.greenburials.org and www.greenburialcouncil.org provide information on green funerals.

FULL BODY BURIAL at SEA Non-Cremated remains may be buried at sea under specified EPA conditions. Please see http://www.epa.gov/region2/water/oceans/burials.htm

CREMATION – The body is reduced to gasses and bone fragments through the use of high temperatures. Also see http://www.cremationsolutions.com.

www.cremation.org is one site that provides information and links to cremation options and providers by state.

BIO-CREMATION (also called Resomation®) – The scientific term for this is Alkaline Hydrolysis, a water/alkali-based alternative to burial and cremation. It is described as a chemical process that results in a highly accelerated version of natural decomposition. After months or years of natural body decomposition, ash (bones) and a liquid remain. Alkaline Hydrolysis yields the same result after only a few hours. Proponents cite energy savings and carbon footprint reduction as key elements in favor of this process.

www.resomation.com, and www.biocremationinfo.com. (This is considered the “green” alternative to cremation.)

Burial and Cremation Options

CASKET FOLLOWED BY CREMATION Some people combine both concepts: An open casket for visitation followed by cremation (or bio-cremation). That option is obviously more expensive than direct cremation, but it is an option!

WHAT TO DO WITH CREMAINS With either cremation or bio-cremation, "ashes" remain, and loved ones will need to know what to do with those remains. (The Cremation Association of North America advises that the term "cremains" is appropriate when referring to cremated human remains.)

The "ashes" are the remains of the larger bones which survive the heat and are pulverized into a consistency that resembles ashes. Pathologically they are inert and can be shipped via any traceable means, including the US Post Office, UPS, Federal Express, etc. Cremation offers a means of transporting the remains far less expensively (and with less paperwork) than transporting a body.

"TRADITIONAL" OPTIONS FOR CREMAINS

Place in a box or urn. And now there are new containers called "scatterboxes." They are designed to allow you to open them from the bottom so you can scatter ashes without "dumping" them from the top.

Scatter them at sea. Both http://ashesatsea.com/ and www.seaservices.com have information.

Scatter them on land. Just make sure it is legal first. For example, scattering on private property without the owner's consent is not legal. Many national and state parks have permit requirements, and location limitations. Talk with your funeral home director or do a quick search on the internet to be sure it is legal.

Inter in the ground (at a cemetery) at a traditional funeral service.

Place them in a columbarium (a wall "vault" found in some houses of worship).

My twin sister's remains are in a columbarium. I love to visit her there... in the peace of the church.

NEW... "INTRIGUING" OPTIONS FOR CREMAINS

We have provided some sites below if you would like further information about these options. Of course, we do not endorse any particular option or providers, but found some of these VERY, VERY interesting. Also, search the topic. More providers may be doing this!

SPACE BURIAL – A small sample of the cremated ashes are launched in a lipstick-size capsule using a rocket. For more information see www.celestis.com, www.heavensabovefireworks.com and www.heavenlyjourneys.com

Burial and Cremation Options

ETERNAL OCEAN REEFS – This is where remains are (in various ways) incorporated into a living reef. We found two ways this is being done so far, but more may be coming!

1. Cremated remains are sealed inside a steel sphere reef ball. The ball is paced in the ocean, to eventually become part of a living reef. www.eternalreefs.com
2. Cremated remains are mixed with non-porous cement and molded. Divers place the molded object within a reef structure. www.nepturnmemorialreef.com

DIAMONDS OR GEMS – These are created from the carbon of a loved one. Some places also offer crystals (bigger than the gems). We found information at www.lifegem.com

PAPERWEIGHTS – Cremains can be included in hand blown glass paperweights. We found information about this at www.cremainsincrystal.com

PORTRAITS FROM ASHES – An artist will create a one-of-a-kind portrait with a special mixture involving oil paint combined with some of your loved one's ashes. Information can be found at www.DustyRoseCremations.com

COMMEMORATIVE TATTOO INK – you can be inked on a loved one! See eHow.com/how_782858_make-tattoo-inks-out-ashes.

STAINED GLASS WINDOW – add a small amount of your cremains large or small. See www.scattering-ashes.co.uk

BIODEGRADABLE COFFINS – a molded recycled paper/mineral shell that will compost the garden. See www.treehugger.com

FIREWORKS – Fireworks displays can actually incorporate remains of a loved one. www.heavensabovefireworks.com

HOURGLASS CREMATION URN KEEPSAKES – both table top and necklace sizes. See www.inthelighturns.com

BE PRESSED INTO A VINYL RECORD – you choose the music and order discs for all your family and friends! See www.andVinyly.com

HUGGABLE TEDDY BEAR URNS-a little stuffed bear with a zipper in his back for your cremains. See perfectmemorials.com

TURN INTO A TREE-compost a seedling and become a tree! See www.bigthink.com

ADDITIONAL IDEAS *Exit Strategy: Thinking Outside the Box* by Michelle Cromer.

I want my remains to be included in a fireworks display during a big party I have planned, hosted by my family!

Burial and Cremation Options

IMPORTANT TIMING (AND $$ SAVING) INFORMATION ABOUT BURIAL AND CREMATION

Direct Burial
In a direct burial, the body is buried shortly after death, usually in a simple casket. The body is taken straight from the place of death to the cemetery or the cremation society. No viewing or visitation is involved, so no embalming is necessary. A memorial service may be held at the graveside or at a later date.

Direct burials generally cost less than traditional funeral services. Burials involving funeral homes can cost $10,000 or more. Direct burials can cost around $2,500 (or so we have been told, but you should call to check).

Direct Cremation
It is not always necessary to send a body to a funeral home before cremation. If you choose Direct Cremation, the body is taken from the place of death straight to the crematory, bypassing a funeral home. (Search your area's cremation society website for information.) You may want to engage a funeral home for other reasons, but if you want to save money and simply cremate the body, it can be taken directly to a crematory.

A memorial service can be held after the cremation. Direct cremation can cost as little as $500 (or so we have been told, but you should call to check).

Types of Services and Gatherings

There are many ways to commemorate someone's life. This is a matter of preference. Some people elect to have simple or quiet events, and some people prefer bigger more public events. This is just like life – we are all different, and you should do what fits you and your loved ones!

THE LINGO

Generally speaking there are options ranging from:

- Gathering to support the family the evening before an official service, burial, or disposal of ashes
- Gathering to support the family the day of the official service, burial, or disposal of ashes
- Private ceremonies/services conducted with or without an officiant
- More open ceremonies/services conducted by an officiant
- Grave-site ceremonies/services conducted by an officiant
- Post grave-site (or disposal of ashes) gatherings

Some are very solemn. Some are very festive. Clearly, this is a matter of personal preference. For the purpose of this book, we have defined the terms below to help you communicate your ideas/wishes with your loved ones. If you prefer different terminology, just modify it or explain your wishes in detail on the pages that follow. Be specific!

VISITATION

This is designed to allow people to gather with the family and share memories. It is generally held in a funeral home or at a church. Often, close friends and family gather informally at someone's home the evening after death. The term Visitation as used here is a more "formal" or "organized" gathering. It is sometimes held the night before a funeral (either a private family funeral or a more "public" one). A Visitation can also be held immediately before a funeral. It can also be held with no funeral at all, simply to give people the chance to visit with family. The body can be in a casket, or the remains in an urn. OR it can be done with no body or remains, just photographs of the loved one.

WAKE

This is a social gathering, similar to a visitation, but is often held in the home or in a "semi-private" nature. It is held the night before a funeral or service. It can include mournful singing, or other music. Sometimes people stay awake all night in theory watching over the decedent. The corpse or remains are sometimes present.

Types of Services and Gatherings

MEMORIAL SERVICE
This is a secular or non-religious funeral, with or without the body of the deceased. In the Orthodox church, it can also refer to a service performed a specific amount of time AFTER the funeral.

FUNERAL SERVICE
This is a formal service conducted by an officiant. It is usually held in a house of worship. It can be held with or without the body of the deceased.

GRAVESIDE SERVICE
This is a service (either religious or secular) performed at the graveside, or wherever the cremated remains are placed.

RECEPTION
This is a gathering after a service. It can be large or small. It often includes food and beverages hosted by the decedent's family.

CELEBRATION OF LIFE
This is more of a festival atmosphere. There is often upbeat music, food, and sometimes dancing. The dress can be casual or more "evening" dress, depending on the time and location. Sometimes this is the ONLY service at all!

I definitely want a Celebration of Life, as well as a traditional funeral service at church, and as of today I'd like my body donated to science with my remains in a columbarium. (I can change my mind, but I feel good about having communicated my wishes!)

Since I plan on a fireworks display with my ashes, the party I've planned includes Kansas City BBQ, jazz, and beer! It will be fun. Donations will be accepted toward a college scholarship I have established in memory of my mom.

My Plan - At A Glance

❑ I have a pre-paid funeral plan with ____

at ______________________________ (address) and __________________ (phone number)

The documents confirming this transaction can be found in the ___________________________

____

❑ I do not have a pre-paid funeral plan.

BURIAL OR CREMATION?

❑ I'd like to be buried (go to page 274)

❑ I'd like to be cremated (go to page 278)

❑ I'd like a casket funeral followed by cremation

SERVICE CHOICES

(Definitions for these services are on pages 271 – 272.)

❑ Wake

❑ Visitation

❑ Memorial Service

❑ Funeral Service

❑ Graveside Service

❑ Reception

❑ Celebration of Life

Even if you have a pre-paid funeral plan, be sure to fill out the appropriate sections of this book so your loved ones do what you WANT them to do! Would that be a first?

My Plan – Burial Preferences

CASKET OR SHROUD (for green or eco-burial)

❑ I've paid for a ❑ casket and a ❑ vault from ______________________________

Their phone number is ______________________________

and their address is ______________________________

____

❑ I have not paid for a ❑ casket and a ❑ vault, but prefer the following style: ______________

____

❑ I prefer a green or eco-burial if it is available. (Simple bio-degradable casket or shroud.)

Here are my thoughts ______________________________

____

FUNERAL PLOT OR CRYPT

❑ I have paid for a funeral plot at ______________________________ (name).

Their phone number is ______________________________

and their address is ______________________________

Documentation can be found in ______________________________

____

____

____

My Plan – Burial Preferences

❑ I have paid for a crypt at ____(name)

Their phone number is ____

and their address is ____

Documentation can be found in ____

____

❑ I have not paid for any burial location, but would like to be buried at ____________________

____(name and address of cemetery)

as close to ____as possible

HEADSTONE OR MARKER

❑ I have paid for a headstone from ____ (name)

Their phone number is ____

and their address is ____

Documentation can be found in ____

The headstone generally looks like __________________ The color is ___________________

and the inscription should be ____________________ (color and font style) _____________

❑ I have not paid for a headstone, but would like one that looks like ______________________

(include color of the stone, shape and font style).____

I would like the following inscription on my headstone: ___________________________________

____

My Plan – Burial Preferences

We found these headstone quotes interesting…

Benjamin Franklin, Christ's Church Burial Grounds, Philadelphia, PA:

The body of B. Franklin, Printer

(Like the Cover of an Old Book
Its Contents torn Out
And Stript of its Lettering and Gilding)
Lies Here, Food for Worms.
But the Work shall not be Lost;
For it will (as he Believ'd) Appear once More
In a New and More Elegant Edition
Revised and Corrected By the Author

Frank Sinatra
"The best is yet to come."

Sonny Bono
"And the beat goes on."

Epitaph in a cemetery near Wetumpka, Ala.
"Here lies the body of Jonathan Blake,
Stepped on the gas instead of the brake."

Gravestone near Uniontown, Pa.
"Here lies John Yeast, Pardon me for not rising."

Cemetary in Ruidoso, N.M.
"Here lies Lester Moore, Four slugs from a forty-four.
No Les, No Moore."

The site www.headstone.net has a lot of headstone and marker information. For types, symbolism, and characteristics, you can go to www.everlifememorials.com/v/headstones.htm. and http://www.iscga.org/memorial-inscriptions-for-gravestones.html.

During one funeral I attended the women's 4-year-old great-grandson placed a toy tractor in her hands so she would have something to play with in heaven. (He also thinks that you get "rocket shoes" when you die and that's how you get to heaven.)

My Plan – Burial Preferences

THE PERSONAL DETAILS ABOUT MY BURIAL

Clothing I'd like to be buried in: ______________________________

____

____

I prefer an ☐ open or ☐ closed casket

I would like to be buried with the following special items: ______________________________

____

____

I would like the remains of my pet ______________________________ (name)

to be buried with me in my casket ______________________________

Flag over the casket? ☐ Yes or ☐ No

Other special burial instructions:

Caskets are available with pockets and drawers, so there are often spaces for special items and notes. Be sure your loved ones know that they may send you away with their final gifts.

My Plan – Cremation Preferences

CREMATION CHOICES

I Prefer ❑ Cremation or ❑ Bio Cremation ______________________________

❑ I've made arrangements with ______________________________ (funeral home)

at ______________________________ (address)

and ______________________________ (phone number)

The urn I have selected is ______________________________ (description)

____

____

Receipts can be found in

❑ have or ❑ have not paid for this.

❑ I have made no cremation arrangements, although I would like to be cremated.

Notes:

If you do not tell people your preferences or ideas, they may find it hard to take action! I have a friend who keeps her parents' remains in her closet! They had burial plots, but moved across the country before they died, and are now both… in a closet!

My Plan – Burial Preferences

I'd like my cremains (also called "ashes") to be: ____________________

❑ Buried at sea.____________________

❑ Scattered ____________________ (if it is legal)

❑ Interred in the ground at ____________________ (cemetery or other location)

❑ Placed in a columbarium at ____________________ (name)

____________________ (address)

❑ Launched into space.____________________

❑ Incorporated into an ocean reef.____________________

❑ Turned into a diamond or diamonds or other gem ____________________(details)

____

❑ Incorporated into a crystal paperweight.____________________

❑ Made into a portrait.____________________

❑ Incorporated into a fireworks display.____________________

❑ Taken home in a box or urn to be ____________________

❑ Given to ____________________for him/her to determine what to do

❑ Other ____________________

____

____

My Plan – Service Wishes

For any service , I love the following types of flowers: ______________________________

____

❑ I am interested in offering people the opportunity to submit gifts in lieu of flowers. Please have them direct the gifts to (list one or multiple):

____

____

❑ I am not interested in gifts in lieu of flowers.

	Music/Songs or Hymns	Written Word (scripture or poems or favorite quotes)	Family Only or Open to Others?
	________	________	________
❑ Wake	________	________	________
❑ Visitation	________	________	________
❑ Memorial Service	________	________	________
❑ Funeral Service	________	________	________
❑ Graveside Service	________	________	________

My Plan – Service Wishes

MUSIC FOR THE SERVICE(S) – THE DETAILS
Consider names of songs and types of instruments or vocalists. If you have specific friends or favorite performers for the music, be sure to mention their names.

PHOTOS I'd like friends and family to see at the service(s):

My Plan – Service Wishes

WRITTEN WORD FOR THE SERVICE(S) – THE DETAIL

Reading	Reader (first and last name)
__________	__________
__________	__________
__________	__________
__________	__________
__________	__________
__________	__________

❑ Be sure to contact the VFW for military services at my funeral. ____________________

❑ I would like the eulogy to be delivered by __________________________ (name)

at ____________________________________ (phone number)

A eulogy is a speech about the deceased. It is meant to be a tribute to the person who has passed. It can be difficult to deliver (emotionally), but it is very meaningful to the family and loved ones.

____

____

____

____

____

My Plan – Service Wishes

❑ Pall Bearers, if I have a casket. (They are often listed as "honorary pall bearers" if there is no casket.) Their names and phone numbers are:

1. ______________________ 5. ______________________

2. ______________________ 6. ______________________

3. ______________________ 7. ______________________

4. ______________________ 8. ______________________

____

❑ Church Bells: ____

❑ Officiant: My preferred officiant is ______________________ (name)

from ______________________ (house of worship name)

Other requests or special instructions for the service(s): ______________________

____

____

____

____

____

Please do not (for the services): ______________________

____

My Plan - Reception or Celebration of Life Wishes

Food	Music (Performers and/or Specific Song Selections)

❑ Reception

❑ Celebration of Life

My Plan - Reception or Celebration of Life Wishes

Other types of entertainment. ______________________________

____

____

____

Photos I'd like friends and family to see at the reception or celebration: ______________________________

____

____

____

Other requests or special instructions for the reception or celebration: ______________________________

____

____

____

____

____

Please do not (for the reception or celebration): ______________________________

____

____

____

Balloon "makers" and magicians performed at the Celebration of Life for one of my friends.

My Obituary

The purpose of an obituary is to inform the public about the death, and give information about the planned funeral and memorial arrangements. They commonly contain: Name, age, place of residence, birth and death dates, and sometimes state the cause of death. Other common elements include surviving relatives, employment history, passions or hobbies. They can and should be as unique as the special person they memorialize!

My birth date, location and my parent's names can be found in the chapter titled It's All About Me. Please be sure to mention the following information I have checked ❑ in my obituary.

❑ Schools I attended, and degrees achieved. This is also in the chapter titled It's All About Me. Be sure to mention the following about my school experience:

____

____

____

____

____

❑ Accomplishments that mattered to me ________________________________

____

____

____

____

____

____

My Obituary

❑ Military Service ____

____

❑ Volunteerism (see the Volunteerism section in It's All About Me for a full list of my activities). Ones that were especially meaningful to me include:

____

____

❑ Other Information (My passions, for example) ____________________________

____

____

❑ The photo I would like included with my obituary can be found ____________________

____

❑ My spouse, children, grandchildren, siblings. (See the chapter titled It's All About Me for my family tree.) While this is one of the most important sections, it is most commonly listed last in an obituary when it states that the loved one is "survived by" (list of names).

________________________ ________________________

________________________ ________________________

________________________ ________________________

________________________ ________________________

________________________ ________________________

________________________ ________________________

My Obituary

Here is some space for a written obituary, if you are so inclined. If you need help or ideas, try websites like www.obituaryguide.com.

The most meaningful obituaries include the person's passions, their goodness, and the things and people they most love.

My Obituary

If you would like to see other obituaries, flip to the "References and Tips" section at the end of this chapter!

Other Information I Want to Share

References and Tips

Tips to Help You — Your Funeral Should Be as Fabulous as You Are!

1. Understand you will be missed, and help those who will miss you!

2. For additional help writing an obituary, go to http://www.ehow.com/how_3456_write-obituary.html and www.legacy.com

3. For more information about planning memorials and funerals, go to http://www.ehow.com/way_5162060_funeral-memorial-planning.html

4. Pre-funding your funeral can be done in two ways: (a) Pre-pay a funeral home or other provider, or (b) Place money into an account for the purpose of your funeral and leave specific instructions to your loved ones.

Take into consideration whether you may move (in which case a pre-paid funeral may not make sense unless your remains will to be sent to that location), and the financial integrity of the funeral home (or financial institution if you choose to place money in a designated bank account).

5. For an historic look at funeral history, visit the National Museum of Funeral History in Houston, Texas. Go to www.nmfh.org for information.

6. Sometimes it helps to read other obituaries. If you know the name of someone who has passed and would like to see their obituary, try www.archives.com. It is currently a free site. We have also found some interesting obituaries in the NY Times. When you read these, you get a feel for the person, the life they lived, and the people who love them.

   www.nytimes.com/2010/10/24/sports/24miles.html
      Honoring Dick Miles, a famous table-tennis player.
   www.nytimes.com/learning/general/onthisday/bday/0928.html
      Fondly remembering Ed Sullivan.
   www.nytimes.com/learning/general/onthisday/bday/0131.html
      Commemorating Jackie Robinson's amazing life.

7. Some people make websites dedicated to honoring the deceased. We reference Bob Chinnery's funeral in various sections of this book. His funeral website is: http://www.speakschapel.com/book-of-memories/352867/Chinnery-Robert-Bob/obituary.php

Examples from Real-Life Fabulous Funerals

One of my great uncles loved cars, motorcycles and airplanes. Motors and wheels were his passion. He designed his own custom casket: candy-apple colors with inset LED lights that changed colors. Four biplanes performed acrobatics over the cemetery. When the planes left, one returned to perform alone – paying tribute to a lost wingman. AND his hearse was pulled by a motorcycle.

Examples from Real-Life Fabulous Funerals

Buck O'Neil, the legendary Negro Leagues baseball player and one of the best men I have ever known, was not eligible for an official military fly-over at his funeral since he had been an enlisted man in the service, where he ironed shirts. Only officers, and particularly those decorated, get special burial privileges. Regrettably he was neither an officer nor decorated, as an undereducated black man in segregated America. Fortunately, he did receive a special Missouri National Guard helicopter fly-over during Taps. The helicopter floated away just as Taps ended. I'll never forget it. It was one of the most moving experiences imaginable, despite my initial skepticism.

Here are some other "elements" we have seen, experienced, or heard about. Each of them helped provide a special personal touch. Everyone deserves to be reminded that their loved ones are special...

- Boy Scouts singing in a circle surrounding the graveside of one of their own, an Eagle Scout who died in high school.
- A bag piper marching over a hill into the sunset.
- Balloons being released at the graveside.
- Doves being released at the graveside.
- Wife singing a song to honor her husband at his Celebration of Life.

A grandchild singing Amazing Grace at her great-grandmother's funeral... My daughter did this!

"Saying good-bye doesn't mean anything. It's the time we spent together that matters. Not how we left it."

Trey Parker

CHAPTER

13

How to Say Goodbye

In this chapter you can say goodbye both personally and from your Virtual Self (online).

Face to Face

Our friend Alison told us about when her step dad was dying. He was not quite with them, but could not seem to pass comfortably. They told him, “It is OK to go. It is all organized. You did just great and we are all happy. We love you.” With those comforting words, he was able to make the transition. Peacefully.

Is there anything that would help comfort you in your transition? If so, write it here so your loved ones can know about it if they have the chance to help you transition face-to-face.

____

____

____

Saying Goodbye

Consider the people you would like to leave some warm thoughts with. What if you die unexpectedly? Are there things you want to be sure people know? Use this page to jot down the names of the people you would like to be sure to say a personal farewell or thank-you.

____

____

____

____

____

Leaving Notes After You Die
Social Media and Virtual You

We can only say "wow"! A few short years ago, there was no social media. Now it is everywhere from Facebook to Pintrest to Twitter and LinkedIn just to name a few. Here is your opportunity to list the social media you participate in/on, and consider whether or not you want people notified on social media after your passing.

FACEBOOK: Have you looked into ways to say goodbye on the social networks? We just found www.ifidie.net. The app utilizes three trusted friends picked by you. Once they confirm your death, facebook will notify your followers. www.facebook.com/help/contact/305593649477238

The TWITTER process is: Support.twitter.com/groups/33-report-violation/topics/122-reporting-violations/articles/87894-now-to-contact-twitter-about-a-deceased-user#

LINKED IN: https://help.linkedin.com/app/answers/detail/a_id/2842/~/deceased-linkedin-member---removing-profile

Beyond Social Media to Online notes:
We just saw www.lastwrite.com where you can leave a note that will be delivered upon your (confirmed) death.

And, www.Deadsoci.al is an opportunity to create a series of messages posted to your social networks when you pass away.

My grandmother left instructions for a bakery to deliver my uncle's favorite cake to him on his birthday after her death.

"A good character is the best tombstone. Those who loved you and were helped by you will remember you when the forget-me-nots have withered. Carve your name on hearts not on marble"

Charles L. Spurgeon

CHAPTER

14

A Quick Checklist for You When I'm Gone

This list should be addressed very soon after death. It's not in required order since so many things must be done simultaneously,

...and because each situation is different, and laws vary by state. Be sure to comply with the laws that apply to your situation.

A Quick Checklist for You When I'm Gone

FIRST THINGS FIRST

ACTION TO TAKE Personal Matters	WHO?	STATUS
THE FIRST STEP If I was a hospital patient, the hospital will begin the process of legally declaring me dead. If I was at home as a hospice patient, contact hospice (if they were not present). If I was not a hospice patient, call the local Emergency Responders (often 911) to notify the local police or sheriff. A coroner or medical examiner will be required to visit the scene if the death was unexpected. They will probably take photographs.		

CHOICES REGARDING MY BODY

Organ Donor

Find my organ donor documentation if it exists, and advise the Emergency Responders or hospital/hospice staff. (Check my driver's license and the chapter in this book titled My Fabulous Funeral.)

At the time I filled this out:

❑ I have an organ donor card or legal document (which can be found in ________________________), or

❑ I do not have an organ donor card or other legal document.

A Quick Checklist for You When I'm Gone

ACTION TO TAKE Personal Matters	WHO?	STATUS
Donation to Science If I have arranged for my body to be donated to science (a medical school for example), immediately advise the Emergency Responders or coroner or other entity if specified in the instruction documentation so the proper process can be followed. The procedure is different than "normal" embalming, and must be managed properly. Again, see the chapter titled My Fabulous Funeral. At the time I filled this out: ❑ I have made arrangements to donate my body to science (documents can be found in ______________________), or ❑ I have not made arrangements to donate my body to science. If I donated my body to science, there may be remains to manage at a later date.		
An Autopsy? In some cases, it will be performed as a matter of course. If it becomes an option, be aware that if the death is accidental, insurers may require an autopsy to prove it was accidental. Also consider whether there may have been medical malpractice leading to the death, an autopsy could help prove that case. When in doubt, call an attorney for guidance here.		

A Quick Checklist for You When I'm Gone

ACTION TO TAKE Personal Matters	**WHO?**	**STATUS**
Call My Best Friends and Relatives… and my Work/Office Friends. Here are their names:	See the chapter titled *My Little Black Book* for their contact information.	

A Quick Checklist for You When I'm Gone

ACTION TO TAKE Personal Matters	WHO?	STATUS
Ask About Bereaved Airline and Hotel Rates		
Call the Funeral Home If the death occurred out of town, notify the funeral home in the decedent's home town. They can make transportation arrangements, see the chapter titled *My Fabulous Funeral*.		
Consider My Wishes, Please Review the chapter in this book titled *My Fabulous Funeral*, or find other documentation regarding my wishes and any plans I have made.		
Keep a List Of calls, flowers, gifts, and people who are helpful in this difficult time.		
Call the Church, Synagogue, or other location to schedule the service or gathering.		
Arrange Hospitality for Visiting Relatives and Friends		

A Quick Checklist for You When I'm Gone

ACTION TO TAKE Personal Matters	WHO?	STATUS
Draft the Obituary and Submit it to the Newspaper(s) There is information in the chapter titled My Fabulous Funeral that will help you. (I may have actually started this for you.) Remember, there are now on-line systems where people can send their wishes to the family. Be sure to ask about those.		
Arrange for a House-Sitter Obituary notices give time and date information. People with bad intentions may plan to make a visit to an empty house.		
Call Pallbearers, Readers, and Musicians If I filled out the My Fabulous Funeral chapter, they will be listed. (see page 259)		
Feed My Pets (instructions starting on page 83)		
Send Thank-You Notes		

A Quick Checklist for You When I'm Gone

BUSINESS MATTERS **Documents to Find!**

- ❑ Social Security Card or Number
- ❑ Veteran's Discharge Papers, Separation, or DD-214
- ❑ Birth Certificate
- ❑ Marriage Certificate
- ❑ Divorce Papers
- ❑ Birth Certificates for Surviving Children
- ❑ Insurance Policies
- ❑ Deeds
- ❑ Title Insurance Policies
- ❑ Any Business Agreements Signed by the Decedent (partnership, franchise, royalty, etc.)
- ❑ Titles (cars, boats, RVs)
- ❑ Mortgage Documents
- ❑ Documentation of Loans I've made
- ❑ Financial Records (including stock certificates, credit card statements, etc.)
- ❑ Tax Returns Filed
- ❑ Will and/or Trust

Other documents I need you to find:

- ❑
- ❑

Keep this list in mind as you go through my papers! Any time you see one of these items, put it in an "Important Document" stack!

If this book has been filled out, you should find guidance about the location of these documents! The following list is the "short" list. The detail can be found in the previous chapters.

A Quick Checklist for You When I'm Gone

ACTION TO TAKE Business Matters	WHO?	STATUS
Call My Attorney(s) See the chapters titled My Little Black Book and Legal Junk for the name(s) regarding my will and trust agreements. I may have listed other attorneys for transactions relating to my assets in the chapters titled Money In and All My Stuff.		
Find My Legal Documents There is a list on the preceeding page called "Documents to Look For." Keep your eyes open for each document in that list. Note: If the will is in a safe deposit box, you may need a court order to access it, depending on the jurisdiction (unless you are authorized to access the box).		
Call My Accountant(s) Their names and numbers can be found in the chapter titled My Little Black Book.		

A Quick Checklist for You When I'm Gone

ACTION TO TAKE Business Matters	WHO?	STATUS
File a Tax Return for the Year of My Death Tax returns will also need to be filed every year after my death until my estate is settled. See www.irs.gov for tax tips/help. • Save all monthly statements (individual and joint accounts) that show the account balance on the date of death. This will be used in the tax return. • You may want to keep my old tax returns in the event the return is audited. (Ask an attorney how many years you should keep on hand.)		
Obtain 10-15 "Original" Death Certificates Contact the coroner, funeral home or crematorium for these. You will need certified copies (not copies from a copy machine) for many purposes.		
Call My Employer Discuss pension plans, credit unions, any death benefits, and insurance. (See "Health Insurance" below if it was provided through my employer.)		

A Quick Checklist for You When I'm Gone

ACTION TO TAKE Business Matters	WHO?	STATUS
Health Insurance Advise the insurer of the date of death and provide any required documentation. Discuss continuing coverage for dependents covered under the policy. Remember, health insurance may cover my hospital and other medical care. The chapter titled Insurance should help you.		
Life Insurance Contact life insurance companies to file a claim in a timely manner. Refer to the chapter titled Insurance.		
Other Insurance Auto, Accidental Death and Dismemberment, Disability, Fire and Casualty to name a few. Some or all of these may need to stay in effect. Be sure to provide notice of death as required by the insurer (certified mail, return receipt requested) in a timely manner. Some may require notice within 30 days for example. You do not want to miss anything that could cause policy cancellation if you need the policy to stay in effect. If the deceased is the beneficiary on any other policy, arrange to have that name removed and replaced. Hopefully I have listed all my insurance policies in the chapter titled Insurance.		

A Quick Checklist for You When I'm Gone

ACTION TO TAKE Business Matters	WHO?	STATUS
Social Security Provide proper notice of death as soon as possible. Payments will cease, but overpayments can result in a time-consuming repayment process. If you are the surviving spouse, ask about your benefit options. Also ask about benefits for any minor children.		
Veteran Benefits Contact the Veteran's Administration if appropriate. You may be able to apply for a burial allowance, a flag, and a government headstone or marker. 800-827-1000. You will need a copy of the discharge papers.		
Credit Card Companies Notify them. Ask if there is any life insurance through the credit card provider. Also discuss closing the accounts. Be sure to advise the credit card company if you, as a survivor on the account, would like to retain the use of the card.		
Notify All Banks Determine how accounts are titled, and how the assets should be managed.		

A Quick Checklist for You When I'm Gone

ACTION TO TAKE Business Matters	WHO?	STATUS
Find the Safe Deposit Box Keys and Safe Combinations The chapter titled *Spy Codes* should help here.		
Find the Assets Find the assets listed in the Money In and Stuff chapters. Be sure to look for "hidden" assets. Hopefully the hiding places are listed on the *Hide and Seek* page of the *Stuff* chapter. Also find any other assets not listed (new bank account statements for example).		
Discontinue Utilities Obviously, only if it makes sense in the dwelling. (You may need to keep the base utilities, and discontinue cable for example.) See the chapter titled *Money Out* for a list.		
Stop Subscriptions and Cancel Cell Phones Consider whether and when to cancel (or forward) cell phones, stop subscriptions to newspapers, magazines, and even the monthly fruit club. Review the list of my expenditures in Money Out to see what makes sense to stop.		

A Quick Checklist for You When I'm Gone

ACTION TO TAKE Business Matters	WHO?	STATUS
Pay Important Bills Like the mortgage. When in doubt about how to handle bills, contact my attorney or hire one. Again, the chapter titled Money Out can be helpful about my "usual" bills.		
Forward the Mail Contact the Post Office to forward my mail. You may need a death certificate and proof that you are administering the estate.		
Notify My Doctors and Pharmacy Just let them know that I am gone. They may need to cancel future appointments or standing pharmaceutical orders. You may need to provide a death certificate.		

Other Actions You Should Take

Additional Tasks

Notes

Notes